# The Position of Women
## In
## Nineteenth-Century English Literature

# The Position of Women
# In
# Nineteenth-Century English Literature

by

Veronica M. Boyle Churchich
B.A. (Hon.), M.Ed.

**VANTAGE PRESS**
New York

Published by Vantage Press, Inc.
516 West 34th Street, New York, New York 10001

Manufactured in the United States of America
ISBN: 0-533-13346-7

Library of Congress Catalog Card No.: 99-96745

0 9 8 7 6 5 4 3 2 1

To my mother Sarah, to whom I owe so much,
and to my ever-patient husband

# CONTENTS

# ACKNOWLEDGMENTS

My special acknowledgments are due to my colleagues in the English department at the Bexley Technical and High School for Girls for encouraging and supporting my decision to write this important work.

I am very grateful to my friend Agnes Rigby, who kindly and diligently read the whole manuscript, for her valuable academic advice. I am also thankful to Dr. Willie Boyle for his helpful assistance in preparing the manuscript.

I wish to thank the University of London Library staff for allowing me to use the books for research connected with this study.

In my general approach to this study, I owe much to the literary tradition represented by positive female and male writers who bravely and triumphantly fought for sexual equality and women's freedom.

# The Position of Women
## In
## Nineteenth-Century English Literature

# INTRODUCTION
# BY DR. NICHOLAS CHURCHICH

Veronica is a child of her benign and cultured background. She was born into a religious home of a gentle, enlightened, well-educated, and erudite family. She has a delightful natural talent and sought neither to conceal it nor to exceed it. Both her parents were distinguished scientists. Her mother Sarah was a well-known, self-disciplined, and successful medical practitioner. Her father John died as a young man when Veronica was only a little girl. She hardly remembers him and, as a result, her mother's memory has always been at the centre of her parental love.

Veronica's mother, being a woman of strong character and very fine feelings, was a deep influence in her life. As a devout Christian, Veronica always thought kindly of her parents, never forgetting their loving kindness and self-sacrifice. Thanks to the determination of her strong-minded mother, Veronica had a splendid education. As a schoolgirl, she exhibited exceptional talents of acquisition, tenacity of memory, and consistent interest in practical performance.

Being a very graceful human being, Veronica has always had the deepest respect for others. She inherited a happy mixture of her parents' characteristics, including piety, humility, hospitality, human dignity, generosity, and magnanimity. Combining brilliant intellect with a very warm heart, she was able to display extraordinary insight into the human psyche. Her sincerity of mind and her refined feelings led her through many absorbing spiritual and social experiences. Veronica's equable temperament, combined with the belief in the equality of the sexes, has helped her to express her intellectual talents in writings.

In Veronica's human world, family stands foremost. She is the only daughter. Being older than her brothers Alan and Tony, she unselfishly supported them during their university education. Their mother encouraged her children to read at home and thus provided a stimulating context for Veronica's writing. Veronica has always shown disposition towards learning and writing. Writing, she says, in A MIND OF HER OWN, gives her the most enjoyment and she hopes that her own writings will have the same effects of her readers.

Veronica received her literary enthusiasm from an intense reading in childhood of the classics and modern writers. Under the influence of her mother, she also read works in the field of science, especially biology and medicine. Veronica, in fact, never ceased to read and study, and her acquirements became extensive and profound. To her, self-culture is fundamental. In Veronica's view, culture means not only the cultivation of some capacities, whether spiritual or physical, but the symmetrical development of all. The keynote of true culture involves the harmonisation of the intellectual, emotional, and volitional elements and must be expressed in the harmony of a complete and single life.

Veronica studied English literature at the University of London, and in addition to the degree of this university, she also holds a diploma in education of Cambridge University. In all her writings, she displays a wide range of knowledge not only of English literature but also of history, philosophy, theology, sociology, and science.

Veronica's writings display a writer of unsuspended strength, a writer with intelligence and a serious, critical purpose. She wrote three novels of which A MIND OF HER OWN is the first and best loved. Here she focuses her mind on the importance of education, morality, and harmonious family life. The stress is on education, which, she thinks, is the main route by which men and women can arrive at the solution of their moral, social, and psychological problems.

Like A MIND OF HER OWN, A DIFFERENT KIND OF PERSON is also about education, teaching, and family life. In ROOM FOR DOUBT, Veronica explores the inner aspects of human personality with special reference to the suffering of a young handicapped girl. Motivated by sympathy, Jenny's parents ultimately decide "to take, in turn, the care of their daughter."

In these three novels and in her ambitious work on THE POSITION OF WOMEN IN NINETEENTH-CENTURY ENGLISH LITERATURE, Veronica touches reality at more points and remains a persistent, irreducible ego.

I have just found Veronica's big script—bigger than that for A MIND OF HER OWN. So far, the title of this Veronica's fifth work is undetected. The main theme is writing as an ideal of meaningful life and a source of self-culture and intellectual enjoyment.

As a teacher at the Bexley Technical High School for Girls, Veronica left the impression on her students of being a very successful pedagogue and their sincere friend. Believing in the influence of good example in the formation of character, in Veronica's view, positive education should be based on moral principles. Man is a natural as well as a spiritual being, and the progressive realisation of the educational and ethical end demands a conformity of the natural to the ethical order. Like Jane Austen, she is well aware "how unfavourable to the character of any young people must be" the totally unethical treatment that they experience at home and in school. The child who has a consistent upbringing clearly has a good opportunity to get the idea of the importance of ethics, while the child who can find no reason on principle in its upbringing may never do so.

Veronica was held in high esteem by all her colleagues at the school. They regarded her as an expert in English literature and well-informed about the position of women in the nineteenth century. Having in mind Veronica's competent and extensive knowledge not merely of English literature but also of sociology, history, and science, they asked her to write on the social status of women in nineteenth-century England as reflected in English literature. Veronica was very pleased with their proposition and responded affirmatively.

Although Veronica gives much prominence to "precious freedom" and "independence" of women in A MIND OF HER OWN, it is in her ambitious work on THE POSITION OF WOMEN IN NINETEENTH CENTURY ENGLISH LITERATURE that she analyzes in some details the whole relation of woman to man, which at the end of the nineteenth century became the subject of scrutiny. In reality, this work is carefully built around a structure of ideas that have always been of the utmost concern to Veronica. It forms a vital link in the logic of her development as a writer. The most remarkable quality in this work is the ever-present touch of objectivity.

The central theme in Veronica's work on THE POSITION OF WOMEN IN NINETEENTH-CENTURY ENGLISH LITERATURE is the liberation of women from the irrational domination of men. There is no doubt in her mind that the position of women in the last century was pathetic and invidious. All social structures were male-dominated. Discussing the attitudes of men towards women, Veronica is definitely in agreement with those writers who intrepidly and indefatigably fought for the independence and "precious freedom" of women. She knows there were mockers and indifferentialists as well as enthusiasts and pioneers.

What all women "of best nature, with good education and strong character" want, Veronica indicates, is their "freedom, equality and independence." These noble ideals, including "professional equality," were denied to them. Many hypocritical writers were satisfied with meaningless observations and empty phraseology but did nothing concretely in respect of "women's freedom." In Sybil, Disraeli uses a woman "to proclaim a course for workers rather than a course for women's rights" (chapter 2). On the whole, Veronica indicates, Victorian "man sees woman as a partner who will further his career rather than humanity" (chapter 1).

There were some writers in Victorian society who believed that women's emancipation and independence were not far away. What was lacking, Veronica agrees with George Eliot, was a concerted effort of writers and reformers to stimulate new consciousness that was needed in the brave struggle for real freedom, equality, and independence of all women.

Veronica belongs to the modern school of thought inspired by Christian philanthropists and pioneered by J. S. Mill, Jane Austen, George Eliot, Charlotte Bronte, and Florence Nightingale. There is no place in her writings for the odious Nietzsche's ideology that "the independence of women is one of the worst developments in the general uglification in Europe." She dismisses Aristotle's low opinion of women and shares the Socratic view that there is no essential difference between the natural endowment of women and men.

In Oriental religions and societies, including Buddhism, Hinduism, and Islam, women are still assigned a secondary religious and social status. In the Koran the stress is laid on unquestioning submission of women to men. Only men have rights, including the right to decide whether to have children or not. In the story of creation in the Old Testament, every sphere of woman's life is dependent on man. This view is reflected in St. Paul's attitude towards women. It is true, he speaks of the equality between "male and female in Christ," but he still clings to the phraseology of the Jewish tradition, which subordinates the female to the male sex. It is not surprising, therefore, that feminists have taken offence at his "false consciousness" about the inferior status of women.

Although Christianity has abolished in principle all man-made distinctions between the sexes, some Christian sects still advocate the intrinsic inferiority of women.

The French writers of the Age of Reason, with the exception of Condorcet, did nothing for the emancipation of women. Rousseau opens his treatise on *The Social Contract* with the famous words that "man is born free but is everywhere in chains." When he speaks of freedom in this context, he means "freedom" from the constraint of advanced political institutions and "perverted society." Freedom from such constraints can only be regained by a return to the lifestyle of the "noble savage." Rousseau is not a feminist. Woman, he says, "is made to please and to be in subjection to man." Like the Muslims, he is not interested either in the liberation of women or in their education. He is pleased that "there are no colleges for girls."

The study of the position of women in social structures dates from the publication of J. J. Bachofen's *Das Mutterrecht* (Mother Right) in 1861. In this work he maintains that matriarchy or the dominance of women in society preceded patriarchy. In his enthusiastic advocacy of the liberation of women, he describes "woman as the repository of all culture, of all benevolence and of all devotion." Influenced by L. H. Morgan's work on *Ancient Society* (1877) and Bachofen's *Das Mutterrecht*, in his work on *The Origin of the Family* (1884) Friedrich Engels confirms Bachofen's belief that matriarchy preceded patriarchy. "The overthrow of mother right," he says, "was the world historical defeat of the female sex. The man took command also in the home and the woman was degraded and reduced to servitude. She became the slave of his lust and a mere instrument for the production of children."

Engels's belief that the dominance of women in society antedated patriarchy has rightly been regarded as a major contribution to the feminist movement. In modern civilised society, the female is no longer seen as merely "the nurse of the embryo" and the male as the only relevant agent in procreation. In the nineteenth century, however, most male writers believed in the intrinsic inferiority of women. In Germany, Hegel thinks that women are capable of education, but they "are not made for activities which demand a universal faculty in the search of truth and knowledge." Bentham shows no interest in mother right. According to Charles Darwin, it is "woman's greater tenderness and unselfishness" that distinguishes her from "man in mental disposition."

In THE POSITION OF WOMEN IN NINETEENTH-CEN-
TURY ENGLISH LITERATURE, Veronica argues that a society must
be judged by the way it treats women. The more willingly men deal
humanly and sympathetically with the female sex, the more disposed
they are to be just, reasonable and social, and less prejudicial, intolerant
and dictatorial. She attributes the low position of women in Victorian
society to the lack of education and to conventions. Dominated by false
consciousness of utilitarian ideologists, the Victorian society, Veronica
indicates, imposed a host of conventions that allowed the strong to
exploit the weak and the rich to exploit the poor.

Edmund Burke favoured the cultivation "in our minds every sort
of generous and honest feeling that belong to our nature," but he never
said anything about the subjection of women and their liberation. Following David Hume, he treated society as an artificial, not natural,
organism. Burke rests his social theory on conventions, which may con-
tain elements of obscure instincts, propensities, and even of prejudices.
He agrees with Hume that justice is the product of conventions. This
uncritical acquiescence of conventional morality, based on the principle
of utility, has been strongly denounced by idealists, social reformers,
and philanthropists.

As a moralist and philanthropist, Veronica has no room in her moral
world either for Benthamite radicalism which eulogised the naked self-
interest and treated society as a fictitious entity or for Spencerian evolutionary utilitarianism, which reduces morality to the struggle for survival. Bentham's and Spencer's moral and political theories are
reactionary. They are based on the belief that human nature is "incur-
ably selfish." Freedom and equality, in their view, must always be determined by the principle of utility, which is identical with self-interest.
Common interest is seen as the expansion of private interest. Obsessed
with the principle of utility, Bentham wants us to believe that utility is
the test of all virtue, of all social strivings, and of liberty.

While many male writers in Victorian society were satisfied with
the ethics of utility and with the policy of *laissez faire*, Veronica, like
George Eliot, has no patience with either. She praises both female and
male writers who maintain that the intellectual and moral perfection
of man and woman is only possible in a free society. A good society,
Veronica thinks, is the society that permits freedom of thought and
opens up the opportunity for satisfying ways of life, not only for men
but also for women. This needs the elimination of evil customs and

prejudices. It needs the progressive transformation of pathetic conventional morality into reflective morality, which offers a wider range of positive freedom.

Customs and conventions vary greatly and certain customs and conventions that were formerly useful are no longer profitable. Many customs and conventions have been detrimental to the welfare of society as a whole. They tended and still tend to perpetuate deploring injustices and superstitions. In different forms conventional ethics is hindering today moral and social progress in many countries in the world. In the Muslim world, religious orthodoxy and customary morality regulate all sexual relations along strongly patriarchal lines, creating, as Max Weber observes, sexual privileges for the wealthy. In this masculine socio-ethical stratification, the position of women is reduced to the position of slaves.

Analysing the position of women in Victorian society, Veronica maintains that conventional morality and utilitarian standards are responsible for the enslavement of the female sex by men. In George Meredith's *The Egoist*, sexual passion is never so important as sexual domination. Willoughby, seeking a certainty through conventions and sentiments, but incapable of real love, gets in the end the dusty answer of losing Clara and marries Laetitia, who no longer adores him.

In Victorian society, utilitarians were in favour of gradual reforms, but on the whole, they clang to traditional "common-sense" morality, which is essentially identical with conventional morality. The development of critical reflection has issued in a widespread tendency among women to call in question the validity of conventional morality. All educated female writers, as Veronica observes, had nothing but contempt for the trammels of convention and utilitarian standards. Moral and social progress, they believed, is the fruit of human wills freely dedicating themselves to the common good and accepting for their task the work of making social relations as egalitarian as possible. Moral and social development, Veronica is convinced, is the product of free men and women, not of class-orientated laws.

The vehement rejection of utilitarian ethics gradually gave way to "positive" freedoms expressed in the liberty of thought, speaking, and writing. Veronica admits that the process of the liberation was slow and irregular. Even at the end of the nineteenth century, woman was still treated by conventions as the weaker sex needing the strength and protection of men. The women writers concerned with the position of women question argued that no society in which woman is regarded as an inferior being can be truly called free. From their point of view, the only freedom that deserves the name is the freedom of pursuing one's own spiritual, moral, intellectual, and social ideals without discriminatory constraints.

The utilitarians were not without morals, but their conception of morality was egoistic, deterministic, hedonistic, and class-oriented. It favoured the rich at the expense of the poor. In the last century, utilitarianism was the spokesman for a single social interest, which it identified with the common interest. Philosophical radicalism advocated by Bentham and evolutionary utilitarianism advocated by Spencer lacked any positive conception of a social good. Like George Eliot, Charlotte Bronte, Elizabeth Gaskell, and Jane Austen, Veronica maintains that freedom is really a social as much as it is an individual conception.

Veronica shares the view of rational intuitionists, aesthetic intuitionists, and idealist philosophers who believe that man and woman are never lone individuals. They live with others, and are dependent on them just as others are dependent on them. Egoistic individualism ignores man's social character and subordinates society to the despotism of free competition. In utilitarian alienated society, man and woman are inevitably strangers to themselves and to others. All social organisations are class-based. What is wrong with utilitarian society, Veronica is convinced, is that each man or woman looks to himself or herself and no one troubles about the rest. Unlike a society in which the individual and common interests are harmoniously interconnected, utilitarian egoistic society is a host of independent men and women held together only by ties of conventional morality and self-interest.

The central principle of Veronica's morality is the mutuality of the relationship between the individual and the social community. The social impulse in human nature, in Veronica's view, is simultaneously a moral impulse. A really liberal society must not tolerate the irrational discrimination between the sexes. It cannot aim at less than to give to all men and women the right to moral self-determination and to the moral dignity that belongs to both sexes. The hedonistic psychology of utilitarians is fundamentally false because human nature is not merely composed of desires aiming at one's own good or pleasure. It is composed of social affections and disinterested impulses that aim at the good of others. It is this conception of human nature that dominates Veronica's moral, social, and political theory.

The central moral idea in Veronica's ethics, as in Thomas Green's and Immanuel Kant's, is respect for all human beings "whether we like them of not." The subordination of women to men is unjust because it violates the dignity of both. The members of a free society must meet as moral equals and treat each other with respect. As a philanthropist, Veronica never departs from the view that individual freedom, self-respect, honesty and integrity are intrinsic goods apart from their contribution to happiness.

Arguing for the intellectual, social, and political independence of women, Veronica believes that many women in Victorian society "felt" to be intellectually superior to men. Like Jane Austen, Charlotte Bronte speaks in *Shirley* of women's ability "to do most things better than men." In *Sybil*, Disraeli describes Arabella as a woman possessing admirable intellectual qualities but lacking a directive "spirit" or common sense. As a result she submitted without a struggle to the arbitrary will of a husband who was intellectually much inferior to her. Her weak character and naïveté "exposed her to his iron selfishness."

Longing for intellectual and social freedom and independence, enlightened female writers were well aware of their "natural equality" and of their "natural rights." Conventional morality, Veronica says, frustrated the realisation of all their noble ends. There were some educated women who, like Mary A. Arnold, were aware of the lack of freedom and of "natural equality" of their sex but were unwilling to fight for their independence. This conservative neutralist position was repudiated by all contemporary female writers fighting for sexual equality and independence.

The position of women in Victorian society was better and more humane than in the previous century but still in some respects medieval. In the sixteenth century, as in the Middle Ages, wife-beating was a recognised right of man in England and was practised without shame by all classes. Marriage was not an affair of personal choice, but as in modern Muslim countries, of family avarice, especially in the upper classes. In Victorian England, these immoral and antisocial practices were discouraged and proscribed, but the position of woman remained remarkably low. It was only at the end of the nineteenth century that the whole relation of woman to man and of man to woman became the subject of close investigation. The change in attitudes in this respect is well expressed in a remarkable outburst of novel-writing by women and about women.

In all her writings, Veronica leaves the impression of total honesty and objectivity, and we are made to feel both her spiritual yearning and her intellectual fortitude. As an educationalist, in A MIND OF HER OWN and also in THE POSITION OF WOMEN IN NINETEENTH-CENTURY ENGLISH LITERATURE, she is concerned with the lack of adequate education for women. Veronica knows that the history of English educational system has been a prolonged and pathetic story of sectarian obstruction, which badly affected especially the education of girls. Nonconformists and Roman Catholics were prevented by law from taking degrees at Oxford and Cambridge, and in many cases, the examinations for those who were allowed to take them were a mockery. In the first half of the nineteenth century, the public schools were unsatisfactory and almost corrupt. The education they offered consisted mainly of the study of Latin.

Education for the lower classes was virtually nonexistent. There were many small private schools often kept by people who had failed in their trade or profession. Some of their teachers could hardly write. There was hardly any provision of education for girls until the middle of the nineteenth century. The foundation of the Girls' Public School Company in 1872 was greeted with much enthusiasm by all women. The University of London was the first in England to open its degree examinations for women in 1878.

The educational system in Victorian society, as Veronica observes, was closely related to the class structure. In THE POSITION OF WOMEN IN NINETEENTH-CENTURY ENGLISH LITERATURE, Veronica attacks ignorance, illiteracy, and pathetic obscurantism, which hindered the education of women and their independence. In the Victorian age, knowledge was seen as a source of power and influence, and on these grounds, it was jealously guarded and protected by a relatively small ideological elite on behalf of male domination.

Many Victorian women, Veronica indicates, had to be satisfied "with second-hand wisdom" and in the atmosphere of false class consciousness had to conform to the irrational standard of male intellectual pseudo-superiority. Veronica is in complete agreement with those educationalists and writers who, like Jane Austen, J. S. Mill, and Matthew Arnold, regard women not only being able of education but also being able of intellectual activities that may even be superior to those of men. With her unflinchingly honest view of life, she repudiates the exclusively masculine discriminatory ideal of social existence and encourages women to challenge and fight for "sexual equality."

In THE POSITION OF WOMEN IN NINETEENTH-CENTURY ENGLISH LITERATURE, Veronica dismisses the idea, favoured by some male writers in Victorian England, that gender roles in society are conditioned by biology. Unlike Thomas Hardy, who believes that the "weaker female sex" is biologically determined by "the inexorable laws of nature"—the idea very much in the air in the second half of the nineteenth century—and that, therefore, there is no point in educating girls at all, Veronica maintains that biology has nothing to do with freedom of thought or, as she calls it, "mental freedom" and social equality. Biology cannot explain social and moral facts. Sex is a biological fact. Monogamy, celibacy, family planning, education, ignorance, illiteracy, inequality, and slavery are social facts and must not be analysed in terms of biology.

The biological explanation of the sexual roles in society, in Veronica's view, is grossly one-sided and can only satisfy those who, like Herbert Spencer and the Social Darwinists, cling to the belief that inequalities among individuals and sexes are "natural" and that morality and sociology are merely a branch of biology. The emphasis placed by Hardy and Meredith—both male writers—on the biological constraints of human nature lends support to the pessimistic view that the human condition is unalterable.

Like Charlotte and Anne Bronte, George Eliot, Elizabeth Gaskell, J. S. Mill, Charles Dickens, and Henrik Ibsen, Veronica rejects "biological reductionism," which together with conventionalism has forced women to remain in unquestioning submission to men. Veronica correctly believes that educational, moral, and sexual roles are structured to a very high degree by the culture of the society, which includes its norms, values, and beliefs. Evolutionary naturalism attempts to explain the origins of culture by reference to their evolutionary presuppositions, not by investigating the culture itself, which is the symmetrical development of the total self.

Culture includes, as Sigmund Freud indicates, all the knowledge and capacity that human beings have acquired in order to control the forces of nature. Unlike the animal, man can act with reflection and from deliberate choice. The action of the animal is a mere immediate reaction to certain stimuli and impulses. Its life is blind and unerring; we do not criticise its impulsive behaviour. The true cause of human activities, Veronica thinks, must be sought within the man himself, in the unique strength of his rational spirit.

In Veronica's conception of human nature, the differences between the sexes have been grossly distorted by egoistic utilitarians who, like Meredith in *The Egoist*, explain these differences in terms of biology. She maintains that the qualities of intellect cannot be explained satisfactorily either in terms of exclusive egoism—the view held by George Meredith, or in terms of evolutionary naturalism—the view voiced by Thomas Hardy. For Veronica, the calculating egoist does not exist in nature but only in a society perverted by evil customs, conventional rules, and false consciousness.

Veronica argues that egoistic naturalism, advocated by Jeremy Bentham, Herbert Spencer, and some other male writers, is false because it is indifferent to moral and social problems. Bentham speaks of a harmony of interests of egoistic individuals, which can only be achieved by legislative coercion. Spencer thinks that moral improvement in merely an extension of the biological concept of adaptation and that social progress depends on the elimination of those who fall behind in the struggle for existence. There is nothing in their writings condemning the irrational subjugation and slavery of women to men and of wives to husbands. In fact, Bentham cares very little for liberty and has a great contempt for human rights.

Veronica criticises Victorian morality for being hypocritical, hedonistic, and grossly egoistical. Men, she says, were more egoistical than women, but women, especially "in higher classes" were more hypocritical than men. Victorian morality was based on the principle that the female is naturally inferior to the male and that, therefore, is made, as Rousseau puts it, "to be in subjection to man." This erroneous conception of women, Veronica argues, must be attributed to the lack of education, religious inhibitions, class proscriptions, misleading assumptions of innate intellectual differences, and to the existing social atomism of the later half of the nineteenth century.

In THE POSITION OF WOMEN IN NINETEENTH-CENTURY ENGLISH LITERATURE, Veronica describes the servitude of women to men in Victorian society with deep sympathy and unflinching honesty. Being alienated by male dominance, women were discouraged from independent activity and were increasingly confined to a private, domestic life. Some women, including Currer Bell, George Eliot, and

Michael Field, who wanted to write effaced their female identities almost subversibly behind male pseudonyms. A repressive social orthodoxy provoked increasingly a melancholy in women's writings and in their struggle for "precious freedom."

Veronica indicates that "the more generous-spirited male writers admitted that some of their own sex aggravated the situation more than necessary." She blames some male writers for their confused and inconsistent attitude towards women. "Having already inveighed against Pope, Congreve and Swift for writing about women as slaves," in *Henry Esmund*, W. Thackeray contradicts himself when he describes "husband's wife as his slave" (chapter 2).

In all her writings, Veronica is concerned with moral problems of character and family life. For her, the role of the family in the moralisation and socialisation process is crucially important. She deplores the fact that "women within the family circles have been unjustly treated by male domestic tyrants" as slaves. Even "witty intellectual" wives, much more intelligent than their husbands, were subordinated to the irrational servitude of their intellectually inferior husbands.

William Wilberforce and his friends succeeded in stopping the slave trade in the British Empire of 1807 and the Act of 1833 abolished slavery, but the slavery of women persisted in different forms throughout the nineteenth century. It is true, wife beating was not a recognised right of man in Victorian society, but it was still practised secretly by the rich and the poor. Within the framework of social and legal rules, the relationship between husbands and wives remained unequivocally ignoble, discriminatory, and degrading. Victorian industrial society offered economic, political, and intellectual independence only to the husband. With the wife tied down at home with cooking and a prolonged involvement in child-bearing, the husband was in reality a major determinant of all family affairs.

Veronica adheres to the view that family life is intensely personal and that it should always be based on the intrinsic value of genuine love, which must be distinguished from sexuality. In her moral world, there is no room for the Eros of antiquity, which dominates Freudian psychology. Genuine love between husband and wife must be grounded on egalitarian principles. This entails that the person loved returns the love. When conceived in this sense, the woman is, as Engels puts it, "on an equal foot" with her husband. Veronica has nothing but praise for "the tendency of some of the so-called weaker sex to stand on their feet" against the domineering role of husbands in the family. Close relationships and harmony in marriage must always depend on honesty, sincerity, patience, and understanding, which, in turn, are inconceivable without "sexual equality."

As a Christian moralist, Veronica condemns adultery, divorce, and abortion. She also proscribes prostitution and illegitimacy, indicating that "the poor classes were more tolerant of these social evils than the rich classes." In *Ruth*, Mrs. Gaskell appeals to her readers to understand "innocent and snow-pure Ruth" because she was seduced at the age of fifteen and knew "nothing of the world of sex." She must be blamed only because "the morals of the young lady reader," as Veronica puts it, "must be protected." All that Ruth needs is our sympathy.

Analysing the problems of spinsterhood in Victorian society, Veronica says that there was a tendency either to ignore it altogether or to regard it as "symptom of emerging freedom." Male writers regarded spinsterhood with contempt. Female writers, by contrast, were sympathetic and more realistic. When Charlotte Bronte wrote *Shirley*, she believed she would never marry. Having pondered much on spinsterhood, she blames utilitarian false consciousness and ignorance. She speaks of the barren lives of unmarried middle-class women, without occupation, without education, with "nothing to expect from society but contempt and despise." "The sole aim of every one of them is to be married but the majority will never marry." The fact that their lives are confined to "household work" and that they are deprived of all "earthly pleasures" is not their fault. It is the fault of utilitarian ideologists, who, like Bentham and Spencer, gave all the rights to men and all the duties to women. Spinsterhood, Veronica indicates, should be viewed with sympathy and good understanding as it reflects alienated social relations.

Veronica shares Charlotte Bronte's criticism of the aridity and misconception of Victorian spinsterhood. Male writers who treated spinsterhood derisively failed to realise that they offended the inward reverence of both men and women as well as the reverence for the humanity that they represent. Being rational beings, both man and woman should be treated as ends in themselves, never merely as means.

Having in mind the despotism of irrational public opinion, many educated women, Veronica says, were perfectly satisfied with remaining unmarried. They preferred to pursue their intellectual interests in freedom. Like men who resisted "to be dictated by women," well-educated women were equally unwilling to be dictated by men. In *The Kellys and the O'Kellys*, Trollope invokes the opinion in this respect of Lady Selina who is not interested in getting married at all. Although a spinster, she is "active, energetic and good as ever; and as ever cold, hard, harsh and dignified." Veronica is in agreement with Jane Austen's observations that "anything is to be preferred or endured rather than marrying without affection."

The problem of marriage and sex is not only an object of concern for the moralist but also for psychologists, biologists, and sociologists. Psychologists are mainly interested in manifestations of sex in human behaviour, including perversions. Biologists study sex from a purely physiological point of view. Sociologists, like moralists, investigate the role of sex in human social relations, which includes family life. Unlike Sigmund Freud and Jeremy Bentham, who believe that the pleasures of sex are preferable to the pleasures of the mind, Veronica rejects hedonistic naturalism and holds that the pleasures of the mind are much superior to those of the body. The natural life of sensibility is not in itself evil, but, she insists, it must be mastered and controlled by the rational spirit.

Veronica has no patience with Freudian psychoanalysis because Freud ignores the importance of the spiritual aspects of human nature. Freud and his followers overlook the fact that sexual dynamics is only one element in human nature. Freud's obsession with sexuality and libido has no place in Veronica's Christian ethics. Like C. G. Jung, she is convinced that human existence is unique in the whole of nature and that the life of mere nature is irrational. The fulness of human life and self-development need the reality of the soul or spirit.

In Veronica's conception of self-culture, moral progress cannot be legitimately divorced from moral values. The graduation and organisation of moral values depend on man's and woman's conscious activities, which are expressed in personal and social life. The realisation of all intrinsic values, like all spiritual and moral aspirations, Veronica insists, is only possible in free society. Restraints are necessary in the interest of order and in the process of harmonisation of different conceptions of liberty, but they are evil and alienating when they discriminate between the rights of men and women. Without equal rights between the sexes, the life of spiritual enrichment of women is necessarily frustrated.

The concept of individual rights was a favourite category of utilitarian writers in the nineteenth century as it is today in the capitalist world. Unlike Kant, who subordinates legal rights to moral rights, utilitarian writers, including Bentham, reduce moral rights to legal rights. Rights, Bentham says, are "not derivable from any other source than law." He treats moral obligations or duties as "fictitious entities," indicating that the only duty man has is the duty to himself. Distinguishing between moral and legal rights, the idealistically minded writers believe that moral rights are antecedent to all positive laws. The unique nature of moral rights, Veronica thinks, lies in the moral law, which is distinguished from positive laws. A moral right relates to deliberate actions, which tend to realise the conscious, best attainable end.

Veronica clings to the view that rights and duties cannot exist outside the moral world and that this world is dependent on consciousness. Duty is not duty unless it is consciously done for the sake of duty. As our freedom and our rights are circumscribed by obligations or duties, Veronica shares the Christian belief that rights and duties are correlates. Of all the rights, the right of free belief and worship and the right of intellectual "precious freedom" are dearest to her.

The moral thinking of utilitarian writers in the nineteenth century is completely coloured by the naturalistic psychology of self-interest. There was a tendency to regard not only rights and duties as "fictitious entities" but also justice. Like Thomas Hobbes, Bentham relates justice to law and "judicature." Where there is no law, there is no justice and no injustice. When Bentham speaks of justice, he above all has in mind respect for the existing conventions and artifices about property. Although justice may be associated with law and conventions, as a Christian moralist, Veronica believes that the word "justice" in the moral sense is immutable and eternal. To her, as to Plato, justice, along with courage, self-control, faith and wisdom, is one of the virtues that constitutes goodness itself.

Veronica rejects the view of egoistic individualists and Social Darvinists who, like some Sophists in ancient Greece, identify justice with power. In opposition to them, she conceives justice as the spirit by which men are animated in the fulfilment of their duties. In a wider sense, justice belongs to the sphere of philanthropy or benevolence. Just as temperance is the presupposition of a true self-culture, so justice is the presupposition of a true philanthropy or benevolence.

The persistent theme in Veronica's THE POSITION OF WOMEN IN NINETEENTH-CENTURY ENGLISH LITERATURE is the reiteration of her belief that individual and social good are coincident and interrelated. In her view, there is no self-contained and self-sufficient human being. Love and respect of others, the natural and generous affections towards the good of all human beings are the necessary condition of self-fulfilment. The permanent element in altruism or philanthropy is the recognition of the moral responsibility of others. This recognition, when ingrained in good characters, involves a recognition of their right to free activity and sexual equality.

Egoism is based on the postulate that each man's and woman's reasons for acting in the social world must arise from self-interest and selfish desires. The egoist treats all human beings as means. He categorically rejects self-sacrifice and any doctrine that preaches self-immolation as a moral virtue or duty. The central point of egoism or selfishness is that it is rational to care about one's own interest but irrational to care about the interests of others. The advocates of "rational selfishness" maintain that the only purpose of human life is the achievement of one's own happiness. Bentham definitely makes the individual interest the basis of the general interest. Philanthropy or charity, he says, is nothing but enlightened egoism. Identifying happiness with pleasure, he argues that the happiness of the individuals is the sole end and standard "in conformity to which each individual ought to fashion his behaviour."

Like Stoicism, Christianity identifies moral goodness with benevolence. In fact, Christianity has initiated a new meaning of love, which is clearly expressed in the commandment "thou shall love thy neighbour as thyself." It is this unselfish love that is the foundation of man's moral and social obligation to others. It is also at the centre of Veronica's conception of philanthropy, of human nature, and of deontology.

Veronica is in sympathy with those Victorian writers who, like George Eliot, Mrs. Gaskell, Charlotte Bronte, Carlyle, and Dickens, advocate social justice and the principle of altruism. To her, possessive individualism, which has reached its *reductio ad absurdum* in Victorian society, is an evil force responsible for pauperism and the suffering of the poor. Veronica sees the inequalities of wealth as the consequence of unjust organisation of social relations, which were distorted by Adam Smith, Jeremy Bentham, Herbert Spencer, and Thomas Malthus. The secret of the economic mechanism, they believed, lies in free competition and free trade.

Malthus was the first to state that human existence depends on a working balance between population and food. He advocated the use of contraceptive measures and the postponement of marriage until the male partner was in a financial position to rear a family. For Malthus,

charity or philanthropy is folly and an encouragement of poverty. Pauperism, he thinks, can only be eliminated by preventing the increase in
birth rate in the lower classes of society. Like Malthus, Spencer shows
no sympathy for the poor, for the sick, for the weak and "for the impru-
dent." Sympathy or althuism, he says, "favours the multiplication of
those worst fitted for existence." In Veronica's moral and social theory,
there is no room either for egoistic utilitarianism advocated by Bentham
or for evolutional utilitarianism pioneered by Spencer. They are equally
hedonistic, naturalistic, and extremely individualistic.

Veronica belongs to the school of thought that believes that morality was not invented yesterday and that, like religion, it has a long history
behind it. Being an aspect of human nature, philanthropy cannot be
derived from—what Bentham calls—self-regarding prudence, which is
his equivalent of "the principle of utility"—or acquired during the process of evolution through "natural selection aided by inherited habit."
Rejecting the identification of the moral and the cosmic process, the
evolutionist T. H. Huxley admits that the doctrine of evolution is unable
to explain the origin of morality. In his opinion, the moral man is not
a product of the cosmic process.

The struggle for existence and the survival of the fittest are the
Darwinian categories that lay beneath Victorian laissez-faire capitalism.
The newly-invigorated capitalism produced a plutocracy as baneful as
any political despotism the world has seen. The citizens of the Victorian
state escaped the serfdom of the feudal state only to fall into the serfdom
of an unlimited and unregulated industrialism. Veronica is in complete
agreement with those writers in the nineteenth century who were very
critical of "baneful capitalism." Society based on free competition, an
ideal of political economists and Social Darvinism, inevitably entails
the division between the poor and the rich. While the rich lived in
luxury, the poor were doomed either to live in squalid conditions or in
workhouses. The Poor Law Amendment Act in 1834, containing elements of Benthamism, abolished the system of poor relief, which became available only through the workhouse. Thomas Malthus
demanded the abolition of the Poor Law altogether. No man, he de-
clared, "has a right to subsistence when his labour will not freely pur-
chase it."

Philanthropists were revolted by the heartlessness of a doctrine that
taught that social evils are inevitable and incurable. Writers like Carlyle,
Dickens, Ruskin, George Eliot, Mrs. Gaskell, and Charlotte Bronte

headed a literary crusade against laissez faire and unregulated industrial-ism. Finally the philosophers and social reformers came to the aid of the humanitarians and philanthropists and provided them with ideas to combat the cruel logic of egoistic individualists.

Veronica has always been sympathetic to the genuinely poor. Like Samuel Clarke, Bishop Butler, and Immanuel Kant, she believes that beneficence is a duty because our self-love cannot be separated from our need to be loved by others. We must, therefore, make ourselves an end for others. As a devout Christian, Veronica holds the view that a true ministry to any human need implies a perfect sympathy and identification of ourselves with the needy one. For many years she has been helping with her donations at least twelve charities. Veronica never departs from the deontological principle that it is our duty to help those in need according to our capacity whether we love them or not.

In their acrimonious criticism of possessive and egoistic individual-ism, Karl Marx and Friedrich Engels blame free competition, which has led to "the accumulation of wealth at one pole of society and a simultaneous accumulation of poverty, slavery, ignorance, brutalisation and moral degradation, at the other pole." They describe the Victorian social system as the most enslavening and the most immoral in human history. They share the belief of Eugene Buret, a Christian French econ-omist, who strongly denounced political economy of Victorian econo-mists, that "the ontology of wealth" is responsible for poverty, social inequality, and class antagonisms.

Veronica has never been an admirer of Marxist atheistic and materi-alistic ideology. There is no room in her world order either for baneful capitalism or for historical materialism. She is in complete sympathy with those writers who, like Eliot, Gaskell, C. Bronte, Carlyle, and Dick-ens, believe in a free society in which social organisation is never an end in itself but is always a means to the attainment of individual self-development and freedom. A good and prosperous society, in Veronica's view, must be made up of men and women who consider the interests of others as well as their own. It is in philanthropy, not in selfishness, that both men and women can find the most effective method of self-culture and autonomy.

Veronica agrees with idealist writers and moralists who hold that moral human beings should never surrender their "inner wealth" to the external wealth. Greater inequalities in wealth are bound to hinder the attainment of social equality and "precious freedom." The Victorian love of money and the restless desire of wealth were dehumanising and reifying both men and women. While money may make us independent of others in respect of possessions, in the long run, money makes us dependent upon itself. Money and wealth, Veronica has never doubted, may give us the power to use the powers of others, but there are numerous cases in which money alienates and enslaves us. Veronica is not against wealth as such. Like Eliot and Carlyle, she insists that all wealth should be treated as a means, never as an end in itself. Riches may ennoble a person's external conditions but never man's and woman's characters.

The distinguishing mark of Veronica's THE POSITION OF WOMEN IN NINETEENTH-CENTURY ENGLISH LITERATURE is her persistent criticism of sexual inequality, ignorance, conventionalism, egoism, intolerance and atheism. Like George Eliot in *Felix Holt*, she realises that the moral, social, and political world is dominated by "two sorts of power." There is a power "to do mischief, to be cruel to the weak, to lie and quarrel," but there is also a power to do good, to help the weak and the poor, to be honest and truthful. Without moral power, knowledge, ability and honesty, a life of complete self-culture is impossible.

Veronica believes that an adequate interpretation of morality depends on the recognition that there is a supreme Ground of goodness as well as of truth. Human beings need "others" and they also need God for their self-fulfilment. It is in and through our relation to God, the perfect good, that the moral ideals can be transcended and completed. Without an ethical God and without a world, invisible to us now but hoped for, as Immanuel Kant confidentially says, "the glorious ideas of morality are indeed objects of approbation and of admiration but cannot be the springs of purpose and action."

As a devout Christian, Veronica regards religion as a nucleus and the basis of culture and good manners. To her, the moral life is an aspect of the religious life and it is impossible to draw a hard line between the two spheres. Like the Brontes, Gaskell, Eliot, and Carlyle, Veronica blames philosophical scepticism, historical materialism, Social Darwinism, and fatalism for giving to the nineteenth century an aura of godlessness. The functional or naturalistic view of religion, which displaced God from the firmament of heaven, has no place in Veronica's teleology.

Jeremy Bentham is both a moral atheist, who was anxious to disprove the "utility" of the belief in an immortal soul, and an ontological atheist, who denied the existence of God and of life beyond the world of material reality. Rejecting all forms of idealism in philosophy, he denies that the mental or spiritual is more certain than the corporeal. Obsessed with egoistic strivings, Bentham rejects asceticism and advocates the practice of homosexuality. His atheism has much in common with the thought of the French materialist philosophers in the Age of Reason.

There is much similarity between Spencer's agnosticism and Bentham's religious radicalism. Both are deterministic and both deny the personality of God. In Veronica's view, the truth of religious experience is bound up with the conviction that God is personal, self-determining, and self-revealing. The personality of God is of cardinal importance because the sense in which God is thought to be personal and ethical determines the whole conception of the religious consciousness in man. There is a wide difference between a personal and an impersonal relationship. Reverence is possible between persons, not between persons and things.

Veronica rejects pantheism and fatalism because both appeal to instincts rather than to reflective thought. While some pantheistic writers approximate to Christian modes of thought and expression, some are distinctly anti-religious. The belief that God is present with the same fulness in a human soul and in a stone is alien to Veronica's conception of Christian religion. The same is the case with fatalism. Fatalism was a dominant feature of the ancient Greek religion and today it permeates the doctrines of the Mohammedan faith and of some Christian sects in which piety is based on mechanical obedience to God.

In *Mary Barton*, Elizabeth Gaskell unflinchingly denies the validity of the fatalistic interpretation of Christian religion. The phrase "Do not grieve, for it cannot be helped" is incompatible with the Christian belief in divine love and free will (chapter 17). While Christianity teaches that we ought to live in conformity to the will of God, it always presupposes the freedom to obey or to fail to obey. Like Gaskell, Veronica thinks that free will in rational beings is not determined. We must be free to act both rationally and irrationally. Without this freedom there could be no responsibility for our actions. All idealist writers, like Aquinas and Kant, recognise freedom even in acting badly. If we were determined by rigid laws of nature, then it is logically impossible that events should be other than they are. Moral freedom, in Veronica's view, cannot mean the liberty of indifference because a will that is indifferent to values would not be a moral will.

Veronica agrees with Elizabeth Gaskell that religious determinism leaves no room for any human agency. It is based on the false analogy that the physical and the psychical processes are identical. In *The Principles of Psychology*, Spencer traces the evolution of psychical phenomena side by side with that of their physical mechanism as he thinks that they are aspects of the same process. Mind and matter are only symbols of an "infinite and eternal Energy from which all things proceed." Spencer's agnosticism and Bentham's atheism ignore the radical difference between the mental and the physical. They fail to realise that determinism is a characteristic of the physical universe and freedom a characteristic of human life as experienced. As a result, human destiny is left to the cruelty of fate.

In the Victorian age, religious determinism, reflected in fatalism, was triumphant, loudly proclaiming the approval of "science" for its dogmas, which served as a useful handmaid to possessive individualism and materialism. Inspired by an exaggerated idea of God's omnipotence, Calvin was convinced that the Christian spirit is compatible with industrialism and possessive individualism. According to Max Weber, Calvinism in its English version is the parent of capitalism. In the economic world, Calvin has done for the bourgeoise of the sixteenth century what Marx has done for the proletariat of the nineteenth. In the religious sphere, Calvinism in England proved to be a destructive force. Its deterministic formulation of predestination led to the individualistic morality and the individualistic morality to the disparagement of the significance of the social fabric, including rights, duties, justice, equality and freedom.

The idea of equality has no place in Calvinism. As in Islam, sexual equality is nonexistent. In fact, the consciousness of election to salvation produced a paralysing fatalism, which treated both man and woman merely as means. It is this consciousness that lies at the basis of the exhortation in *Mary Barton* "Do not grieve, for it cannot be helped." There is an assumption that human beings are helpless and entirely left to the indomitable will of the Almighty. The decisive point here for the Puritans is, as Max Weber puts it, a matter of "either or—either the will of God or the vanity of His creatures."

Veronica, like Elizabeth Gaskell, has no doubt that spiritual determinism with its fatalistic elements offers no alternative explanation of the intense sense of freedom that men and women possess or of the will itself, which, according to determinism, is an illusion. By obliterating the goodness of God, fatalism is unable to offer any alternative explanation of such psychical and mental facts as sympathy, humanity, mercy, grief and, above all, as Veronica indicates, remorse, which is "only a darker name for man's conviction of his own free will."

There are things in the moral and religious world that make the soul hopeful and there are things that make it exceedingly sorrowful. Most religious people who, like Veronica, strive to be dispassionate will agree that the truth lies neither in extreme pessimism nor in extreme optimism. The exhortation "Do not grieve, for it cannot be helped" in *Mary Barton* must be rejected because it ignores the fact that man is not a mere instrument in the divine hands, a passive vehicle of the energy of God. Like Gaskell, Eliot, the Brontes, and Carlyle, Veronica recognises the existence of evil but nonetheless her faith is indissolubly linked with hope.

As an intellectual, Veronica is well-aware that no knowledge is complete and that religious knowledge has its limitations. Mystery is never absent from religion. Because of our mental limitations, the purpose of the existence of suffering and death cannot but remain a mystery. Although the philosophy of religion may be able to clarify certain points of our beliefs, it is, however, on the assurance of faith, not on logical demonstration, that religious truths must be based. Veronica knows that the process of rationalising can never be complete and that the exercise of reason is inevitably based on postulates that cannot be rationally deduced.

While admitting that philosophy may play a constructive role in the inquiry into the nature and validity of knowledge, Veronica gives more prominence to faith. Christian faith and love of God and of all men and women are central to her deontology, teleology, and eschatology. Charity is an essential condition of all truly Christian goodness. Dignity and honesty are absolute inner worth that is invulnerable to social relations of power and subordination. It is honesty and rationality that distinguish human action from animal behaviour. Veronica shares George Eliot's view that political power should always be based on "knowledge and honesty." Shocked by the inhuman doctrines of the utilitarians, John Ruskin also insisted that politics should be based on honesty. While honest politics, he says, relates to the laws of life, unrestrained competition relates to "the laws of death."

Veronica is not a sympathiser of Adam Smith who believes that the capitalists are the most intelligent and most industrious class in the community and that "civil government is instituted for the defence of the rich against the poor." She unflinchingly dismisses the political theories of both possessive and evolutional individualism because they are based on the principles of unregulated industrialism and commercialism, naked self-interest, and evident inequality. In *Sybil*, Disraeli speaks of "bands of stalwart men, wet with toil," "troups of youth of both sexes, of infants, many of them girls"—all jobless and victims of poverty.

The assumption that economics and politics are mutually independent, or are only indirectly related in the harmonisation of private and public interests, is one of the most characteristic elements in egoistic individualism. While Aristotle and Aquinas cling to the view that the spheres of the moralist and the sphere of the statesman cannot be separated and that government is "the rule of equals over equals," political economists reduce everything to the laws of economics—to fetishism or the worship of money. This policy produced the industrial proletariat, which gradually became a political force to be reckoned with. Throughout the nineteenth century, many workers were so dissatisfied with their conditions in Britain that they were willing to find a more satisfactory existence abroad.

In Victorian society, self-interest or egoism was, as many writers, including Meredith, Carlyle, Gaskell, and Eliot, indicate, the only principle of morals and legislation. This principle was at the heart of political and economic behaviour of bourgeois political economists in England in the nineteenth century. Unlike the Cambridge Platonists, Richard Price and John Ruskin, who subordinate human laws to divine laws, all utilitarian writers reject the validity of supernatural law and stress the importance of man-made laws, which in fact are always the expression of the will of the ruling classes. In the feudal period, law expressed the interests of the owners of land; in the nineteenth century, it expressed the interests of the holders of industrial capital. Only some intelligent male and female writers—to use Veronica's phraseology—were courageous enough to ask whether the rules of conduct prescribed by the bourgeois ideologists were sensible or stupid, fair or tyrannical, just or unjust, and whether they represented a reciprocal "fitting of needs" and economic interests.

Reducing all spheres of human life to "jurisprudence," Jeremy Bentham substituted the human lawgiver in place of God. The distrust of idealist deontology and its subordination to the test of utilitarian consequentionalism are some of the principal aims of Bentham's jurisprudence. Indicating that "the end justifies the means," he advises the legislator to use coercion whenever necessary to "harmonise" self-interest and common interest. In fact, the harmonisation he has in mind amounts to the reduction, as he admits, of the common interest to self-interest. It is this Bentham's legalistic utilitarianism, as Veronica indicates, that was responsible for "the suffering of the poor," sex inequality, unemployment, class discrimination, social evils and class struggles. Bentham, of course, had support from bourgeois economists, Social Darwinists, and agnostics who, like Herbert Spencer, believed that "socialism" or any form of "egalitarianism" involves "slavery."

The policy of free competition expounded by utilitarian economists became progressively impossible in the second half of the nineteenth century. There was, as Veronica indicates, "a democratic virus at work," the awakening of social conscience to the evils of unrestricted competition of industry. Writers, poets, and reformers helped to rouse public opinion and working-class consciousness. Carlyle wrote bitterly of "the liberty to die of starvation." In *Mary Barton*, Elizabeth Gaskell writes about the suffering of the poor and innocent, their efforts to help one another, their successes and tragedies connected with "the indifferent cruelty of the so-called economic laws." In the Preface she declares she "knows nothing of political Economy or the theories of trade." This ignorance does not prevent her to describe and condemn the heartless cruelty of utilitarian economic laws.

Veronica, like Elizabeth Gaskell, has a deep sympathy "for the care-worn men and women" who have no alternative but to struggle "through their lives in strange alternations between work and want." As a philanthropist, she holds unflinchingly that it is our duty to help those in need. In Bentham's and Spencer's egoistic utilitarianism, there is no place for philanthropy. Spencer makes disparaging remarks about "ardent philanthropy." His belief that "a creature not energetic enough to maintain itself must die" is repugnant to all conscientious men and women. His inhumanity reflects the uncharitable doctrines of English Puritanism and Social Darwinism.

Veronica is in complete agreement with George Eliot that without fellow-feeling, honesty, and decency "no political measures can benefit us." The hardships in the lot of working men and women, the elimination of poverty, the fair distribution of wealth, just organisation of social relations, and the harmonisation of private and common interests are complex problems whose solution requires fellow-feeling or philanthropy in the place of selfishness and knowledge in the place of ignorance. Political measures and economic laws of utilitarian ideologists in Victorian society were undemocratic, male-constructed, class-orientated, and grossly unequitable.

The impulse of altruism and the practice of philanthropy existed, as E. Westernmarck shows, in all primitive societies. In Rabbinical literature, almsgiving was identified with "righteousness" in general and in Christianity, charity or unlimited open-handedness became a cardinal virtue. In the name of the majestic and inexorable laws of an omnipotent Providence, puritan extremists and reformers rejected all previous notions of philanthropy and subordinated them to the economic virtues. In opposition to "economic morality," Veronica, like Elizabeth Gaskell, George Eliot, and Thomas Carlyle, describes pauperism as a social phenomenon. The poor, in her view, are not a class apart but victims of an inhuman social and economic dislocation.

In THE POSITION OF WOMEN IN NINETEENTH-CEN-TURY ENGLISH LITERATURE, Veronica brings into focus moral, social, and political issues that psychologically and materially determine the kind of society that is acceptable to most men and women. These issues centre around education, family life, freedom, sexual equality, class orientation, rights and duties. The peculiar charms of this work lies in its objectivity. As an expert in English literature, Veronica knows her subjects and is in no uncertainty what she wants to say. She grasps precisely her relation to her predecessors and her contemporaries. She writes about what she, as a teacher and writer, has experienced, read, thought and discussed. Her work typifies the spirit of independence, of self-reliance and of confident knowledge of literary developments in nineteenth-century England.

The society Veronica depicts was moulded by utilitarian egoistic individualism, philosophical radicalism, and egoistic naturalism. Its ruling classes identified their own selfish interests with the interests and well-being of the whole community. Like George Eliot, Elizabeth Gaskell, and Thomas Carlyle, Veronica condemns the serfdom of an unregulated industrialism and unrestricted competition because they are responsible for social evils, pauperism, mammonism, agnosticism, inequitable economic laws and sex inequality.

THE POSITION OF WOMEN IN NINETEENTH-CENTURY ENGLISH LITERATURE bears striking testimony to Veronica's knowledge, informed intellectual and moral experience, and scholarly insight. She writes clearly, selects shrewdly, and recollects faithfully. She knows where she stands in the complex analysis of discordant attitudes and interests of male and female writers in the class-divided society. Veronica's analysis is based on the facts as she understands them, and she reads into them nothing that is not there. As a moral realist, she synthesises the messages and attitudes of male and female writers towards women's position in the intellectual world and fuses them into one quintessential whole.

As an intellectual, Veronica focuses her attention in THE POSITION OF WOMEN IN NINETEENTH-CENTURY ENGLISH LITERATURE on the independence of women and their "precious freedom." Unlike male writers in Victorian society who regarded women not only physically weaker but also intellectually inferior, Veronica shares the view of those female writers who believed that women's intellectual capacities in 'most things' and activities are superior to men's. She criticises narrow-minded male writers for their complacent vulgarity and their blind observance of conventional rules of human conduct.

Unlike writers in nineteenth-century England, Veronica has lived enough to see that her noble ideals of women's independence, sex equality and 'precious freedom' became real facts of experience. The question of women's voting rights or suffrage proved to be most difficult to resolve. Women's suffrage was first advocated in England by Mary Wollstonecraft in her book *A Vindication of the Rights of Women* (1792) and was demanded by the Chartist movement in the 1840s. It was also demanded by J. S. Mill and his wife Harriet. The Reform Bill of 1867 contained no provision for women's suffrage but, as a result, women's suffrage societies were formed in most major cities of Britain.

The first country to grant to women the right to vote in national elections is New Zealand (1893). Britain lagged behind many countries in this respect. The Act of 1917 granted to women aged 30 and over the right to vote but it was only the Act of 1928 that lowered the voting age of women to 21 thus placing women on an equal footing with the male voters.

The struggle for the independence of women and sex equality was, like any struggle, a prolonged and painful process. It ended, as Veronica indicates, triumphantly in the realisation of all those noble ideas for which female writers and their male friends fought so bravely.

Veronica's ambitious work on THE POSITION OF WOMEN IN NINETEENTH-CENTURY ENGLISH LITERATURE represents a high level of accomplishment in writing. She always had a deep desire for writing. Like Charlotte Bronte, she thinks that writing is 'the highest and the loveliest pleasure' in intellectual life. It is also an aspect of self-realisation.

Veronica wanted to continue writing. Sadly, malevolent and ignorant practitioners of the art of healing frustrated her noble desire to pursue writing as her principal educational and intellectual aim. Their maltreatment of kind-hearted and medically-conscious Veronica, based on—what Carl Jung calls—the psychology without the soul, is responsible for her unexpected and tragic death. Veronica was buried in January 1998, in Hither Green Cemetery, London, near her beloved home.

Veronica ought to be remembered as a sincere thinker in whose character there is not a trace of self-seeking or self-display. There is much of religious and moral strength and greatness in Veronica's character that deserves our admiration. She is the very incarnation of integrity. Upright, conscientious, and transparently honest in word and deed, she has always governed her life, even in its minutest details, by the highest principles of honesty, decency, moral rectitude, and justice. In addition to being a genuine seeker of truth and knowledge, Veronica has always showed a splendid zeal for great causes and charitable work.

In my mind Veronica will always remain as an exemplary Christian, a conscientious educationalist, magnanimous teacher, an enlightened writer, a valiant champion of the liberation of women from the irrational domination by men and a brave advocate of "sex equality" and "precious freedom" of women. As Veronica's husband and because I share with her spiritual, moral, social, educational and academic ideals of life, I am now losing after her tragic death her admirable companionship, her edifying moral and intellectual support, and, above all, her charitable, affectionate, and very lovely personality.

Veronica grew naturally into a keen understanding of human character. Everyone recognises in her a woman of great character and personality. As an intellectual, she understood perfectly well the importance of moral practice in private life. As a Christian moralist, Veronica has always been courageous in faith as well as in practice, in thought and action—always placing a bigger emphasis on "doing" and on actual human practice.

# PREFACE
# BY VERONICA M. BOYLE CHURCHICH

As a reader and teacher of English literature for a considerable number of years, I became increasingly interested in the status of women writers and gender roles in nineteenth-century English literature. With the tenacious support of my colleagues in the English department at my school, I wrote the present work. Its primary aim is to provide a systematic frame-work to which wider reading could be related.

Literature is not entirely a product of individual genius but also partly a product of social and intellectual conditions. It is the product of a society that has consciously attained a definite moral, social, political, and intellectual advance and is convinced that its new standards of life are superior to those of the previous age.

No writer—male or female—can separate the idea of literature and its direction from the idea of a definite social function or purpose. It is difficult to believe that the favour of readers would remain indefinitely attached to books in which there is little to learn about relevant moral and social problems or in which our religious and moral feelings are denigrated and despised.

Gender roles in literature, as in any branch of culture, are always structured to a very high degree by the norms, values, and beliefs of human individuals composing society. The position of women in society is a sure clue to the forms of freedom it enjoys, if any, and the indication of its maturity.

Social tension over women's position and gender roles in English society developed during the seventeenth century when religious, moral, and political strains increased considerably. This tension had its alienating reverberations in the nineteenth century. It is generally admitted that the lot of women in that century was barbarous and primitive.

Victorian society, it must be stressed, was male-dominated and class-conscious. Whole ranges of behaviour—social, political, and economic—were based on conventional rules and ordinances and were manipulated by men in support of their dominant position in society. Segregated roles in Victorian society were particularly characteristic of working-class families. Some men regarded their wives mainly as providers of sexual and cooking services.

Lack of education, gender-orientated conventions, religious and class proscriptions or inhibitions and fabricated assumptions of innate incapacities and genetic traits inevitably created social barriers between the sexes and affected attitudes of male and female writers towards writing.

As the nineteenth century proceeded, a more independently feminine voice and a more open criticism of segregated roles in the literary sphere became apparent. The effects of social movements, including the Women's Liberation Movement, gradually changed perceptions and legitimations of women as an oppressed class. They also shifted the boundaries of social intercourse and generated a new consciousness of independence.

The end of the nineteenth century witnessed a remarkable outburst of novels written by women and about women. This new vigorous production of literary works by female writers was the first sign of an activity that is familiar to us today.

Thanks to the pioneering work of such writers as Mary Wollstonecraft, Frances Nightingale, J. S. Mill and his wife Harriet, Henrik Ibsen, Jane Austen, Charlotte Bronte, Elizabeth Gaskell, and George Eliot, women have won their independence and freedom. After a prolonged struggle, the Act of 1928 enfranchised all women in Britain and put them on the same footing with male voters. Sex equality, the noble ideal of all women, at last became indubious reality.

# CHAPTER 1

# THE ATTITUDE OF MEN TOWARDS WOMEN IN NINETEENTH-CENTURY ENGLISH LITERATURE

I would like to consider, naturally, the attitude of both male authors and male characters and, as the latter invade the pages of both women and men authors, I will discuss the topics as they arrive and not in two "groups."

In *The Way We Live Now*, Anthony Trollope shows us a grudging admiration of Mrs. Hurtle, partly because she is an American and has had to face things inconceivable to an English woman. She has had to shoot a man in Oregon because he had attempted to rape her and, earlier, kept her drunken husband forcibly from her bedroom (it is presumed with the same gun!). Nevertheless, Roger Carbury remarks to Paul, "Then what must she be, to be here with you? And what must you be, to be here with her in public? People live in such a way now that I don't comprehend it."

Roger knows that Paul has been engaged to Mrs. Hurtle in the past, but since he is now engaged to Hetta, he must avoid even innocent contact with a "doubtful" lady. Such doubtfulness has many shades in men's minds and, although a certain amount of spirited wit was longed for in the future partners of the more intelligent males, the appearance, at least, of total innocence, if not naïveté must accompany such wit.

That a woman might be better off without marriage rather than be tied unhappily, does not cross the mind of many male authors. In "On the Western Circuit" (from *Life's Little Ironies*), Thomas Hardy puts into the mouth of Edith Harnham the words "Influenced by the belief of British parents that a bad marriage, with its aversions, is better than free womanhood with its interests, dignity and leisure. . . ." These may be said to be Hardy's reflections on her need for a lover rather than his real belief that total freedom of identity was what she pined for.

George Meredith had a clearer concept of what a free soul might need in *Diana of the Crossways*. When the heroine talks over her friendship with Lord Danborough, she states, "He was never a dishonorable friend" but goes on to give an interesting description of how much a man can be friendly with a woman without damaging his reputation yet still it would damage hers. This is not a value-judgment on Meredith's part. He obviously burns with the same indignation as Diana herself.

Meredith shows the same empathy in *Rhoda Fleming* when he depicts Ayrton's irritation over the sufferings of Dahlia. "Are not women the flowers which decorate sublunary life? It is really irritating for them to be pieces of machinery that—creak, stick, threaten convulsions and are tragic and stir us in the wrong way?" One notes the deep irony of juxtaposing "convulsions" and "tragic" and the male irritability hinted at in "stir us." Robert Fleming, although characteristically desirous of "taming" a woman, does sincerely admire Rhoda's character. "Devil is what I want in a woman! I can make something out of a girl with a temper like yours." Not the sort of remark every woman wants to hear in the twentieth-century but in the context of the story far more endearing than Edward Ayrton who first seduces Dahlia and then deeply resents her unsuitability as a lively companion!

Once a couple are married, one is introduced to the idea that women have more spirit or more awkward stubbornness than a male bargains for. Obviously a female author finds this "bitter bit" aspect more amusing than does a male author, although Trollope in a relaxed mood or Hardy in a softened one can see the funny side. To illustrate the feminine glee let us take George Eliot's reflections on Lydgate. Before marriage he ponders on the . . . "innate submissiveness of the goose . . . corresponding to the strength of the gander." Later he is to think of her use of tears "As if she was a member of another and enfeebled species." Nevertheless "*she had mastered him.*" Of course, both Lydgate's devotion to study and his over-idealisation of women has led him into this situation, for we are to read later that he is amazed "Dorothea has a fountain of friendship towards men, a man can make a friend of her."

Trollope is obviously mocking men as well as society when he indicates there is nothing of the "The feast of reason and the flow of soul" between Griselda and Dumlello but adds sadly: "How many men can truly assert that they ever enjoy connubial flows or that such flows and feasts are necessary?" True, the marriage of these two in *Framley*

*Parsonage* is but a parody, but like most parodies, it is based on the hard truth of loveless marriages for wealth. Marriages for love do not, of course, necessarily bring the Victorian heroine "flow of spirit." Leaving aside that Dora did not seem to discover any potential spirit until she was dying, David Copperfield had not courted her in search of it.

However, in *Edwin Drood*, Mr. Grewgious states in a rather oblique manner to Edwin that he "Would not like to see him make a plaything of a treasure" and, speaking of Rosa again, Neville remarks to Mr. Crisparkle that he could not bear to see her "treated like a doll." That Rosa by her childlike behaviour has asked, seemingly, to be treated like a doll could be objected, but Edwin has not been adult enough to see that her early orphaned state, together with her many doting friends, have protected her in a strange manner from real life. When they eventually agree to part, Edwin broods to himself silently "It is with some misgiving of his own unworthiness that he thinks of her and of what they might have been to each other if he had set a higher value on her."

Given a woman of spirit as a possible partner, even the most enlightened hero sees her as one who will further his career, even if this may mean a desire to help humanity, as in the case of Felix Holt. "I wonder if the subtle measuring of forces would ever come to measuring the force there would be in one beautiful woman whose mind was as noble—who made a man's passion for her rush in one current with all the great aims of his life." This is sincerely felt by him, but one wonders if George Eliot is a little tongue-in-cheek when one recalls how Dorothea's "great aims" are to be stifled by marriage to Casaubon. Of woman's lack of freedom in marriage, however, I will speak in another chapter.

The political novels of Trollope naturally show us a considerable amount of behind the throne arm-twisting on the part of wives. The Duke of Omnium loves his wife, allows her complete rule in household matters, but "it was intolerable to him that she should seek to interfere with him in affairs of a public nature." Of course, being the woman she is, she continues to do so. Her creator obviously feels that her high rank gives her certain latitude. What is more, he finds her very amusing, intelligent, often extremely kind—if sometimes misguidedly so—yet, all in all, one senses his feeling that she is not really a nice woman! She does not veer between the "naughty" and the "wicked" as does Lizzie Eustace; far from it. But she is not what every good man wants beside his fireside. What, then, do heroes and/or male authors really want? Thackeray seems as satisfied as Pendennis with their Laura (although it took several infatuations to find the right direction!) To a modern reader, she certainly seems a sensible, well-read girl, who gets her own way without the usual mealy-mouthed approach to a husband's whims—but to the same reader, she may seem painfully puritanical in her judgments at times. Still, if an average Victorian professional man can be happy with her, it is an improvement on several other fictional marriages. In *The Warden*, Sir Abraham Hazard is satirised as "Never quarreling with his wife but never talked to her"!

The power of money and inherited business ability is something to be reckoned with in viewing a woman. The men surrounding Shirley may have wished her father had begotten a son, but they are "stuck with" her, and we have to think carefully before we decide that her charm was a large contributing factor. It helped, certainly, but character was much at work also. In Chapter 20 we hear Shirley's own reflections, made to Caroline: "If men could only see us as we really are, they would be a little amazed, the acutest men are often a delusion about women . . . their good woman is a queer thing, half doll, half angel; their bad woman also always a friend." She continues by satirising the poetic creations of such men who produce women "as false as the roses in my best bonnet here." Miss Dunstable in *Framley Parsonage* has a good fortune and can understand business affairs more acutely than Shirley, naturally, as she has a lifetime of experience, but having a male creator she is not described so sympathetically. Certain frank remarks are reported in a lively manner, certainly, and her horror of being married for money is admired both by Trollope and by her few worthwhile friends, but one wonders, again, if charm is assumed to be essential for a woman to get away with being at all manlike (for lack of a more flattering epithet!). In other words, Shirley's youth, wit, and marriageability are talismen that take her a long way.

"Reputation" was all-important in men's eyes in weighing up a woman. Advanced as Hardy would like his heroines to be, he is sadly aware that the contemporary male had a very limited view, on the whole. When his aunt suggests to Wildeve that a second deferment of Thomasin's marriage would "ruin her character," he answers sharply, "Nonsense: that wouldn't ruin Thomasin." But the implication is that unconsciously, over the years, the girl has already built up her "good reputation." Meanwhile, Paula in the *Laodicean*—ever anxious as she is to be modern, enlightened, and free—knows that she dare not "venture on the game of eyes with a lover in public; well-knowing that every moment

of such indulgence overnight might mean an hour's sneer by the indulged gentleman next day, when weighing womanhood by the cool
light of the day and a bad headache."

Paula may be a little harsh here, as much probably depended on
the nature of the gentleman and a great deal (as we saw with Thomasin)
on the character the lady had already built up for herself. As one will
see in other chapters of this book, *Diane of the Crossways* acted in her
friendships as if reputation did not matter as long as one held oneself
in good esteem. But Meredith's view of life was often a challenging one.

Sadly, even his characters had to settle for reputation—or extreme
unhappiness. Even a most enlightened author would resort to the protection of a good husband for the more extremely wilful heroines!

To turn from "ladies and gentlemen," a working man can be shown
as shrinking from "fallen women," but if his character is at all worthwhile, he does not do so when the individual case is one he understands.
In chapter 30 of *Rhoda Fleming*, Robert has "No false sensations" peculiar to men, concerning the purity of women, which is a "false sentimen-
tality of such that can be too eager in the chase of corruption when the
occasion demands." In *Mary Barton*, Jem Wilson does shrink from Esther's approach, but once he realises it is Mary's long-lost aunt, he speaks
to her naturally and with genuine compassion. "Come home with me.
Come to my mother. She and my Aunt Alice live together. I will see
they give you a welcome." Alas! We deduce from her reply that she
does not expect the women to be so charitable!

Although Mr. Varden thinks very highly of Mrs. Rudge and has the
opportunity to study her through much adversity, on her side, he still
remarks ruefully, "I wouldn't have the presumption to say I understand
any woman!" Dickens may well be speaking for himself, but even seemingly enlightened male authors make some strange deductions. Take
the case of Eustacia Vye. Admittedly one who wallows in emotions
and the analysing thereof, but is it likely that any human beings would
deliberately make themselves unhappy by falling in love? Women may
risk such unhappiness because they are passionate by nature, but any
man may do likewise! Yet we read "To court their own discomfiture is
a common instinct with certain perfervid women" (*Return of the Native*,
chapter 6, Part 2). I may be generalising, but it appears to me that
another woman would realise that such a girl cannot live without sensation, but a longing for unhappiness is not part of the package! Male
characters have often just as weird concepts. Through various volumes

we pursue Pendennis as an increasingly acerbic, witty, perceptive young man—often, as he matures, only thinly disguising Trollope himself. Yet when he adulates Laura he says to her that "Some women seem exempt from the Fall. Love, you know, but knowledge of evil is kept from you" (*Pendennis,* chapter 71).

Laura has been telling him that he mustn't belittle himself and in the circumstances given this is very forebearing of her. But this doesn't make her particularly unaware of the evils of the world—swift as we have found her in condemning Lizzie Eustace, for instance. The reasons given for a woman's marrying also seem to indicate a lack of depth, or else a tendency to generalise in male writers. The passage in *Barchester Towers* where Emily is described as clinging, creeping, depending for succour on the departed Mr. Bold, is often quoted, but we find him at the same game in *Rachel Ray* (Trollope, chapter 1). "A woman in want of a wall against which to nail herself (i.e., Mrs. Ray is a widow) will swear conjugal obedience sometimes to her cook, sometimes to her grandchild—to her lawyer"!

Of course all this can be true of some women in the twentieth-century also, but surely throughout history there have been some men who likewise either married for a leaning-post or are in spirit married to their mothers or their cooks? In a darker vein, we see Jude sadly berating Sue for her lack of logic (Part 6, chapter 3) and later for her inconsistencies (*Ibid,* chapter 10). Both of these failings he attributes to her sex and yet throughout *Jude the Obscure* she has been consistent until suffering of the deepest kind made her return to Phillotson. "Strange difference of sex, that time and circumstance, which enlarges the views of most men, narrow the views of women almost invariably." Whether Hardy himself has thrown an ironic reflection on Jude into this remark is left to the reader, but one cannot picture the Brontes or George Eliot attributing such a *volte-face* as Sue's to sex in particular. It could be argued that their heroines do not get themselves into the same messes as poor Sue. However their heroines change their attitudes or their behaviour, the causation is mainly human rather than feminine.

That male authors understand very well what is required by men from women has been mentioned earlier, but the fairest comment one can make is that they may lament their own sex's limitations in so doing. To give two examples: In *The Three Clerks,* Trollope comments: "Katie's beauty spoke to the intelligence, and required for its full appreciation an exercise of the mental faculties as well as the animal senses" (chapter 33).

There seems a rather passive role here for Katie, surely! Yet one supposes that Trollope is aware that men could only be discerning within the limitations of their upbringing and surroundings. By contrast we have Ferdinand Lopez, whose judgment neither male or female reader would trust, but still Trollope seems to be a little sorry for him in that he showed all that was lover-like in his treatment of his new wife, and yet she shows little wifely respect! "Perhaps a rougher manner, with some little touch of marital self-assertation, might have been a safer commencement of married life." Trollope goes on to point out that had she married Arthur Fletcher, he would have been asking her to fetch his slippers by this time! (*The Prime Minister*, chapter 25). Emily, we are told, knows of this tendency and would have "enjoyed his behests" if in the first place "her heart had followed his image." This seems to beg the question, as Arthur's longings for "a sweet servitor" do not seem to be much use to him, if he isn't to win her heart until she has need of more stalwart services and genuine friendship. To look at things from Ferdinand's point of view, we hear a little later that he did love Emily (as well as her money!) and had she "helped him a little more with his devices, fallen into his plans—and made herself one with him "then he could have removed her from her father's influence, gone abroad with her" and returned to his way of "making the world soft for her." In fact Emily cannot win if she attempts to think for herself (chapter 68).

George Eliot reflects in *Middlemarch* that men do not care to see women worshipping their husbands. "Such weakness is pleasant to no man but to the husband in question" (chapter 21). This may be a true observation on the author's part but yet may still arise from a male thinking how foolish old so-and-so is to even appear to deserve such "adoration." On the whole they would expect it from their own present or prospective brides. The word "worship" is rather over-worked from both sides; one must also remember "spoilt loved females and brides seem to look for it from their male wooers. So men may not have looked for it too long after the honeymoon." Certainly in Dorothea's case, disillusion was to set in soon after this chapter.

As soon as one feels one has put one's finger on what the Victorian male really looks for and admires in a woman, one comes across as many diverse possibilities as, frankly, one would today: different ones, of course, but just as varied. The sort of thing one would not come across today would be a eulogy of this sort: "A good woman is the loveliest flower that blooms under heaven—is it not a pity to see them bowed down by Death or Grief. . . . We (i.e., men) may deserve grief—but why should these be unhappy?" (Thackeray, *Pendennis*, Book 1, chapter 60). And this from the lips of a hero who is given to feel he is worldly and cynical. As women were great novel-readers, it is only to be hoped that tastes were not being courted in this way!

Other chapters will seek to show how women behaved and reacted and it may gradually emerge whether some were "their own worst enemies" in any struggle for freedom or whether the majority were fighting a battle which might seem to be a losing one at the time but was gradually gaining ground. Individuality will be found in plenty, but conscious pioneers for emancipation may not perhaps have attracted great authors except from the corner of their eyes, so to speak.

# CHAPTER 2

# TOWARDS SEXUAL EQUALITY

A sad note is often struck by male and female author alike on this theme. It is as if to say "This is the terrible lot of women—alas and a lack that biology should so decree that it should be so!" The more generous-spirited male writer admits that some of their own sex aggravate the situation more than necessary. Most angry female writers would hint that there was much a man might do to control his dominant tendencies—but few of their sex suggest that an equal balance of power in a family or marriage could be struck.

Take, for instance, Thackeray in *Henry Esmond*, Part 1, chapter 11. Having already inveighed against Pope, Congreve, and Swift for writing about women as slaves (and in the latter case treating them as such), he goes on, "Much of the quarrels and hatred which arise between married people come, in my mind, from the husband's rage and revolt that his slave and bedfellow who is minister to all his wishes—is his superior." Individual cases of a woman's "superiority" of character over some complete rogue hardly win any battles in the war of the sexes. Beatrix's outcry in the same book (Part 3, chapter 3) rings more true. Infuriated by the accusation that she is "worldly," she cries out "I have ten times his (Frank, her brother) brains and had I worn a sword and periwig—I would have made our name talked about."

In the same way, Hetty Lambert longs to go to war, quoting Tasso to Henry Warrington to show that she would have no fear. "You men fancy we women are good for nothing but to make puddings or stitch samplers. Why wasn't I born a man I say!" (Thackeray: *The Virginians*, Pt. 1, chapter 62).

Hetty is to show even more anger when George Washington gives up Hetty's sister Theo because his mother demands it of her father "for honour's sake" because Theo is so poor and George has his way to make in the world. "Honour! And you are the men who pretend to be our superiors—and it is we who are to respect and admire you—men who are our superiors in courage and wisdom—I despise you all! You are our betters, are you?" (*Virginians*, Part 2, chapter 76). Laura is frequently sarcastic concerning the position of the sexes. Early in *Pendennis*, when he irritably remarks that she is always (morally) superior to him, she teases, "What, superior to the great Arthur! How can it be possible? You can't mean any woman is your equal?" (Thackeray, Part 1, chapter 27). At a much later stage, Pendennis, now married to Laura, asks her how she knows that Clara, Barnes Newcome's wife, is not so artless as she appears. She again mocks him. "The inferior animals have instinct, you know," and he adds ruefully: 'I must say my wife is always very satirical upon this point of the relative rank of the sexes.' (Thackeray, *The Newcomes*. chapter 69).

Various examples could and will, later in this chapter, be given of admission that individual men are not superior to their mates or daughters, but what is less easy to find is any admission, even by women, that they are not themselves inferior in some way. It is easy to say that Mrs. Gaskell is merely mocking men when she makes Paul's father remark regarding Phyllis: "She'll forget 'em (i.e., Latin and Greek) when she has a household of children." Certainly the speaker admits to admiring Phyllis's intelligence, but when Paul is worried about marrying someone wiser than himself, then any implied superiority must go by the board! In *The Hand of Ethelberta*, although the heroine feels she cannot marry Mountjoy without telling him of her low caste, it doesn't even strike her that he should tell her of his past moral lapses. It could be argued one supposes that this is merely social usage, rather than arising from the relative position of the sexes just as any attempts to be manly (or perhaps merely to enjoy oneself!) were frowned upon in a woman by even a worldly creature such as Foker in *Pendennis*. He refers to Lady Bullfinch as a "horse-godmother" because he has seen her "At cover with a cigar in her face." This is from the insipid youth who dotes on Blanche for all the wrong reason and who has made no comment on the over-rouged actress in an earlier chapter who was also smoking a cigar! The right to smoke a cigar on or off a horse is neither here-nor there, but what we are trying to discover is whether women genuinely felt themselves inferior or whether they merely realised convention limited them and that education was only for blue-stockings—while secretly feeling "equal" in every way. That some women both at that time and in this century <u>felt</u> or wish to <u>feel</u> superior to men is not the aim of this research. Such a feeling merely moves the balance, is frequently illusory, and above all depends on to whom one is comparing oneself: and by what criterion of perfection one is judging!

In *The Egoist* one is struck by Clara's longing for freedom to be herself. She senses Willoughby, despite his looks and charm, is inferior, but if she could be more free, that would not be the question at issue. The sense of being trapped is brought out in the phrase "captured woman" and later "bondwoman." Clara later cries out "My mind is my own, married or not!" When De Craye hears the tone of loathing in which she is to cry "Marriage!", he rather melodramatically thinks he "recognises the virginal cries of someone feeling trapped."

Meredith states more plainly on a later page "Crowned and undiademed ladies of intrepid independence can be like men in being egoists" but goes on to hint that the times have not yet come when women are hunting positively for men so their egoism is not yet on trial (chapter 23). In the following chapter, Clara is to be horrified by her father swaying back to her lover's side by the latter's possession and possible gift to him of a "great wine." Clara muses with disgust "And these are they by whom women are to be abused for variability! Only the most imperious reasons, never mean trifles, move women, thought she—" This is all very fine, but she, or Meredith himself for the tone of the reported speech is not clear, spoils it all by "AND . . . women must respect men. They necessarily respect a father." Yet if there is little in either her lover or father to respect, why must she flee from the house to "spare" her father any showdown? Could she not have enough faith in her own dignity, which would at least be the beginnings of equality? Willoughby himself is inconsistent because although he recalls Constantia as a "bundle of femininity" in her boring lack of individuality and remembers Clara's "individuality as a woman," yet he dreads talking to Vernon lest he receive from him "A phillipic upon women's rights!" Jilted by two women, the chastened Willoughby is to marry Laetitia, who has loved him all along.

Willoughby praises her intellect to her face as a "pearl", and Meredith concludes the novel wryly. "But he had the lady with the brains! He had: and he was to learn the nature of that possession in the woman who is our wife." This would sound sinister as if she is going to browbeat him forever or get round him in various tricky ways. We know Laetitia has no sense of "equality" because of these brains—certainly she no longer worships him and tells him so frequently as the story draws to a close. Yet, she accepts him during their significant talk in the library. "The tutored tone of sentimental deference of the towering male"—it is she who uses this phrase in her mind, it is she who wonders if "it was this which had wrecked him with Miss Middleton." Willoughby senses that this line is not going down very well with her and tries one or two other numbers. Basically, she accepts him because she feels sorry for him and because she cannot get over what has often been called the habit of loving. Throughout she still seems to lack any sense of her own equality and this, no doubt, will enable him to live with the "brains."

*Diana of the Crossways* is probably striving more actively for equality than some heroines, but she is often very self-conscious about it. Her friend Emma smiles at a passage in a letter in which Diana speaks of a "disengaged intellect" implying one without any sexual restraint. The reason Emma smiles is that most reviewers sense a woman behind the assumed name of her writings and there is no need to strive to write like a man to achieve independence. Mr. Braddock, the lawyer in Diana's divorce case, says "he expects the day to come when women will be encouraged to work at crafts and professions for their independence. This, too, is quoted in a letter to Emma, and here Diana does see things more clearly as she adds, "That is the secret of the opinion of us at the moment—our dependence." As her character grows, we are to read that her moral courage makes her more like a man. It "made the endurance of torture a support such as the pride of being is to men." She has, of course, done wrong in Dacier's eyes by giving information concerning him to a newspaper, but he makes her suffer too much for this. As Meredith is to say, nearer the end of the story, we will only like her if we accept that "She never sentimentalises publicly and has no dolly-dolly compliance and muses on actual life and fatigues with the exercise of brains, and is, in sooth, alien." Alien no doubt in that she had fought, sometimes only feebly, sometimes too fiercely, to be herself and had become equal to any man in her battle for life.

There is another kind of equality, which is distasteful to men and only endurable to women if of the same mould—the stridently bossy variety of female who seems to rest quite happily in the pages of literature and, therefore, must have got away with a lot in real life. I am thinking of a creation such as Thackeray's Rachel Warrington. She "quarrelled with those she loved best and exercised over them her wayward, jealousies and imperious humours until they were not sorry to leave her." (*The Virginians*, part 1, chapter 13). Yet as a young bride and mother, when all went her way (for she had been a spoilt child), she no doubt had been as coy, submissive, or even loving as the next maiden. Admittedly this is a historical novel and pre-Victorian eras produced a racier breed of females, but Thackeray's tone suggests that his contemporary readers will be well-used to such behaviour among older women. Remember, too, that it was not just a family and a household of servants she was running, but Virginian estates and many complicated business affairs. Perhaps, if she could have been less dominant with her sons, some attempt at true equality would have been made and she would have been a less lonely old lady. On the other hand, were sons in the habit of treating their widowed mothers in an "equal" manner and had she seen too much lavender and lace treatment of her acquaintances to square it with her own wilful nature?

One must not stray too far from equality of opportunity—the only worthwhile right—in order to quibble too much over equality of nature, although some aspects of the latter must lead to "potential" and if this is recognised, the opportunities can be less easy to refuse. Lord Lufton remarks regarding the "unprotected young ladies all about the world" that he does not find them a bore as Lucy sarcastically suggests he might. "No, I like it. The more I can get out of old-fashioned grooves the better I am pleased" (Trollope: *Framley Parsonage*.) Later Lucy remarks: "I have liked the feeling of independence with which I have thought I could indulge in an open friendship with such a one as you." This refers to his rank and to the fact that love has not been hitherto mentioned between them and she cannot stoop to be thought, by his mother, to be inferior to him. Hetta Carbury has been taught by her mother that "every vice must be forgiven in a man and in a son though every virtue was expected from a woman and especially from a daughter" (*The Way We Live Now*.) She resents this but she is completely restricted financially by her parents from doing anything about it.

In *Eustace Diamonds*, we read a more pungent note. "Is it not the fate of women to play the tunes which men dictate—except in some rare case in which the woman can make herself the dictator?" (chapter 76). Yet neither remark suggests that women have any right to equality. It appears to be something that turns up, accidentally, if you are in the right circumstances or have a very forceful character. Hetta's mother only feels a certain equality with her editor after she has refused him in marriage. "There was certainly between them now more of the intimacy of real friendship than had ever existed in early days. He spoke to her more freely about his own affairs and she would speak to him with some attempt at truth" (chapter 52.) Lady Carbury has developed the habit of lying to Mr. Browne to gloss over her son's dissipated character.

In *The Eustace Diamonds*, Lizzie reflects: "What makes me sure that all this fuss about making men and women all the same must be wrong is that men can get along without women and women can't without men." It is a relief to hear that there was "all this fuss" going on and remember Lizzie was very clever so that, although she spent most of her time cajoling men for financial gain, she could soon have used her wits for other purposes in a modern times. Or would she? Perhaps Lizzie had a lazy streak and preferred using her wiles to sorting out her business affairs of which she was quite capable when driven by necessity.

Sarcasm from a wife to a husband regarding a woman's inequality has already been mentioned in the case of Pendennis and Laura, but one suspects affectionate teasing was more the tone as they are still young and, moreover, Laura has known Pen in a sisterly capacity when they were both children.

The tone alters however in *Rachel Ray*. Mrs. Tappitt refused to be "put down" in discussing the brewery with her husband." Why wasn't I told all this before?" And when he shouts indignantly, "Woman!" she answers soundly, "Yes; woman indeed! I suppose I am a woman and have no voice in anything—" When he more or less tells her to go to the devil, she retorts firmly, "It's clear enough you are no longer yourself and that someone must take up your affairs and manage them for you." She is very loyal to her daughters about their father's need to "retire" but is obviously quite sufficiently confident of her own way with her husband being the most sensible. She does not, in other words, suffer from any sense of being inferior to her husband, nor if she were properly instructed, is she incapable of business skills.

Dorothea Ray (the widowed Mrs. Pryme) feels a great curiosity about "The rights of a married woman with regard to money—and also the wrongs—but we may say this of her, let her have asked whom she would (i.e., for advice), she would at least have been guided by her own judgment." Mrs. Pryme is considering a second marriage and is not over-eager that her money should be taken over by a future husband, whatever the law. She is not always a pleasant woman, but at least she indicated a tendency for some of the so-called weaker sex to stand on their own feet.

Class caused strange deviations from the norm also. For instance, Mrs. Yeobright gives the (male) peasants a very hard stare or rather one of "unconcern" because, being a curate's daughter, she feels it is not the business of those of a lower caste to ponder why she walks alone at night (Hardy: *Return of the Native*, chapter 3, Book 1).

A reader might comment that this has little to do with any feeling of sexual equality but merely with the general snobbishness of the Victorian. In answer, one would point out that Mrs. Yeobridge has brought up her son with great strength of character and financial struggle and were she to mix more with society would soon, no doubt, have extended her indifference to certain mores to all ranks of society.

Her daughter-in-law is to demonstrate a struggle for understanding on a much deeper level when she pleads in a way what a man should hear for her comparative innocence in the death of Clymn's mother. "I confess that I wilfully did not undo the door the first time (*Return of the Native*, chapter 3, book 5) but I should have opened it the second if I had not thought you had gone to commit bad faults sometimes." It seems to emerge from these reflections that women with any sense, good education or strong character longed to be free but had not necessarily seen this as a freedom to the city of equality with men — but merely freedom from dominance — just as an over-dominated child may long to leave home but does not in any way feel this will make him inferior or superior to his parents. In other words, many women in literature seem to have a quiet awareness of their "natural" equality but just don't know where to begin to achieve professional equality. We will see in a later chapter what professions or trades lay open for women and what educational facilities lay open for them. Even in the political novels such as *Sybil*, we see that Disraeli uses a woman to proclaim a "cause," but it is really the workers' cause as a whole rather than a plea for women's rights. I have headed this chapter "Towards Sexual Equality" and the stress is on the first word — whatever was happening in historical fact. We read that many writers seem to have preferred exposing and talking about the enslavement, and the consciousness thereof, rather than any signs of the freeing of women.

Sexual roles are always structured by the culture of the relevant society that reflects its normative expectations. In every society culture defines the rules that pattern the relations between men and women, husbands and wives. There have always been considerable variations in connection with these relations. In the patriarchal family, the relationship between men and women was more egalitarian than in modern times. There is sufficient evidence to support the belief that the position of women in primitive communal society deteriorated with the advent of class society. The division of labour between the sexes was then reciprocal.

Inequality in all its forms is a persistent feature of societies with private ownership of productive resources and market economies. Equality implies fundamentally a certain levelling, uniform, and homogenous process. It also implies that adequate opportunities are laid open to all members of society regardless of sex. Sex should not determine the legal rights of men and women. Sex, sexuality, and reproduction are all closely interwoven into the fabric of human life, which is best expressed in the family.

There are still some societies today in which women are treated as slaves. In most modern civilised societies, women are equal because they are not seen different any more. In nineteenth-century England, the position of women was far from being satisfactory. All social structures were male-dominated. Egoistic utilitarianism, with its strong individualistic instincts, was too powerful to be easily swamped by writers and novelists who indefatigably fought for the liberation and independence of women. To utilitarian ruling classes in England, the question whether women were equal to men did not arise at all because men proved to be the successful guardians of social structures based on the principle of egoistical calculation. In their view, rights, duties and equality are fictitious entities, which, as Bentham puts it, belong to "the field of law." In fact, it is Benthamine conception of law that is "fictitious." The only social role of his law is to "force" people to be "free."

Status dichotomies and hierarchies confer honour on some and dishonour on others, and in doing so, they legitimise differences and authorise inequality. This definitely was the trend in nineteenth-century England in which the differing perspectives of consensus and conflict were most apparent. The opponents of egoistic utilitarianism held an overall view of society that emphasised equal opportunity for men and women and the absence of class antagonism.

The ruling class in nineteenth-century England represented a single interest, the interest of the rich bourgeoisie. All social structures were dominated by men and the woman was a mere instrument in male-dominated society.

Victorian society was based on the principle of commercial free-dom or *laissez faire* responsible for class antagonism and for the low position of women. While man in that society was alienated from him-self and from his fellow men, woman in addition was alienated from the opposite sex and kept in servitude. Many educated women believed correctly that women are not only naturally equal to men but also that they may be intellectually superior.

Male-dominated society in Victorian England propagated the pseudo-biological doctrine that sexual equality is biologically deter-mined. This doctrine was advocated by Social Darwinists and played an important role in Herbert Spencer's egoistic individualism. Spencer glorified the individualism of his age and modelled his society on its pattern. Modern biology denies the view that sexual equality and free-dom are linked with "genetic endowment"; they are rather moulded by other internal and external factors, including social relations.

All female writers in nineteenth-century England rejected the ten-dentious biological interpretation of sexual equality. As the century pro-ceeds, a more independently feminine voice becomes apparent. A repressive utilitarian orthodoxy provoked a reaction among female writ-ers and educated women, encouraging them to fight for sexual equality and independence.

In *Jane Eyre*, Charlotte Bronte dismisses the ideologically-con-structed male supremacy and confronts man as an equal. In *Mid-dlemarch*, George Eliot speaks of the subtle movement of social "vicissitudes which are constantly shifting the boundaries of social inter-course, and begetting new consciousness of independence." While the male writers were engaged in romantic adventurism, the female writers focused their attention on realities, including sexual equality and wom-en's independence. Without the resentment of female writers and edu-cated women to the deplorable position of women in Victorian society, the relationship between men and women could not have become the subject of public scrutiny before the end of the century. Protagonists of the Women's Liberation movement helped to rouse the social con-science and public sympathy for the course of sexual equality and wom-en's independence.

Many writers, philosophers, and scientists, including Charles Dar-win, believe that it is man's egotism that motivates him to dominate the opposite sex. Man, Darwin says, "delights in competition, and this leads to ambition which passes too easily into selfishness." Woman is regarded as a gracious, amicable, and amiable being. In George Meredith's novels, sexual domination is more important than sexual passion. This attitude of male domination must be rejected. Social unity cannot be maintained through the differentiation of the social functions of the sexes. Women must be allowed to realise their own capacities as free individuals.

# CHAPTER 3

## THE INTELLECTUAL POTENTIAL AND EDUCATION OF WOMEN IN THE NINETEENTH CENTURY

There is no need to reiterate what is so often stressed in books on Victorian education that girls' chances were very limited. Home education was the best if you had an astute father, a well-stocked library, and above all the desire to learn. The shallowness of boarding schools for those who could afford them or of board schools for those who couldn't give way, as the century progressed, to the pressures of really worthwhile teachers. All this has been said again and again—but what we will be studying in this chapter is how far women felt good education or natural intelligence made their lives deeper and more stimulating and how far men felt these gifts were a handicap or a drawback in the women in their families, wives or merely the women they came across in society.

In *Middlemarch,* we come across many references to Dorothea's feelings of inadequacy when faced with what she thinks is Casaubon's great intellect. In the early days of his courtship, he laid before her the schema of his "Key to Mythology" and we read "Dorothea was altogether captivated by the wide embrace of this conception. Here was something beyond the shallows of ladies' school literature: here was a living Bossuet, whose work would reconcile complete knowledge with devoted piety" (chapter 3).

Now, no man, unless pursuing Casaubon's field, would at this stage spot these deficiencies, so we can but admire Dorothea's intelligent grasp of his exposé so far. What is touching is that she also realises how her educational background has let her down. In chapter 7 she has moved a step further "—she had not reached that point of renunciation at which she would be satisfied with having a wise husband; she wished, poor child, to be wise herself." George Eliot is obviously reflecting ironically here that many Victorian women not only had to be content with second-hand wisdom but were content that it was so. Considerably later she is to use that intelligence against her husband although longing to be loyal. "You showed me the rows of notebooks—you often spoke of them—but I have never heard speak of the writing that is to be published. Those were very simple facts and my judgment went no further" (chapter 20). Alas, Dorothea's "judgment" went to the heart of the matter. No education prepared her for this, no previous mixing with great scholars, no natural malice or suspiciousness—just plain acuteness. One could speak at length on Dorothea's gradual awakening and her tendency to self-education, but some Victorian readers may have dismissed this as a pen-portrait of George Eliot herself cast in a more immature and naive mould—and therefore a freak, not often to be found in the ranks of real life. Thus let us turn to a male writer, for fairness' sake.

In Trollope's *The Way We Live Now*, Henrietta is questioned by her mother as to her pursuits in the evening. "I have been trying to work hard at Dante but one never does good when one has to try to work" (chapter 39). The second half of the remark suggests she has not been intellectually trained (as her mother has concentrated all her interest and finances on Felix) but, on the other hand, how many modern girls would attempt the interest without the scholastic background?

To take another case: in *Life's Little Ironies* "An Imaginative Woman" Hardy depicts Ella Marchmill as writing verses, not perhaps of a very high standard but nevertheless published. She strangely falls in love with a poet in whose room she sleeps though she never meets him and when she is dying, she cries out bitterly to her husband, "I thought perhaps you weren't up to my intellectual level—I wanted a fuller appreciation, perhaps, rather than a lover." Not perhaps modern emancipation as she needs male recognition of her intelligence, but perhaps if she had developed her creative art, while unmarried, things would have been different? Sordid to need money as backing, but how many men might also give up if they couldn't keep themselves, even if self-appreciation may be (doubtfully) enough for them? Harriet in *A Few Crusted Characters* by the same author is a proud young woman and not much to be admired in her treatment of Jack Winters, but she bases her contempt on his illiterate speaking and style. She told him plainly that she was town-bred and he was not sufficiently educated to please her" (*The Winters and the Palmleys*). This is not altogether a matter of class-distinction as they are semi-engaged and it is only when he goes away to work for their future that his letters antagonise her.

Not a pleasant young woman, but we cannot search only among the "heroines" for signs of longings for a higher education in themselves or their future mates! Take Lizzie Eustace—poor Lord Eustace who had always felt his life would be enriched by contact with a clever woman, who is moved to rapture by her poetry reading. Because she is not a feeling woman, Trollope is to hint later that she "was false and pretentious—making up her mark of literature at the easiest cost of trouble" (chapter 1, *Eustace Diamonds*). But this does not mean she despised learning when divorced from artistic appreciation! She had studied much, she spoke French, understood Italian, read German—of things to be learned by reading she knew much, having really taken diligent trouble with herself" (chapter 2).

In the same novel, Lucy Morris reads *Pride and Prejudice* and the novels of Maria Edgeworth with ease, and Trollope seems to assume that this is part of a young girl's achievements; nothing outstanding. In the same way when Lady Linlithgow asks Lucy if she can do accounts, she answers merrily, "Oh yes! I consider myself quite a ready reckoner!" (Lady L. is asking this of an employee, be it under the disguise of a companion, so she literally "means business"). Should marriage not mature for Lucy, she will contemplate life as a governess as unbearable but necessary for independence. As lord Lufton's affianced, she is persuaded to see this would be lowering. Although being a companion to a lady is excrutiatingly boring to her, she will accept it. So here, again we obviously have the mores of a person who is well-educated for her day but without any drive to be anything but a good wife or an "enduring" spinster! Mrs. Vincy regards teaching as akin to shop-keeping. "An intimacy with Lindley Murray and Mangnall's Questions," she says, is "something like a draper's discrimination of calico trademarks. No woman who was better off needed that sort of thing" (George Eliot, in *Middlemarch*, Book 3, chapter 23). She was referring to Mrs. Garth, who had been a teacher before she was married and therefore was to be despised for "earning her bread"! Yet Mrs. Garth still teaches individual pupils at home and appears to enjoy it although obviously money is a stimulus for the needs of her family. In A *Laodicean*, chapter 6, Part 2, Paula would not allow men to watch her as she is dressed in boys' costume for the exercises, but it is still very advanced of her to have a gymnasium built: "She holds advanced views on social and other matters and on those on the higher education of women she is very strong, talking about the physical training of the Greeks—so she had the place built in imitation of those at the new Colleges for women." Admittedly, *Middlemarch* was written in 1872 and Hardy's novel in 1881, but a decade cannot change attitudes so much. Mrs. Garth worked to help out her husband and often felt a little irritated by *having* to work (although basically enjoying the work); Paula, critics might point out, was in a sense of dilettante in that she had money and may have been playing with ideas. Yet do not both men and women in this century work for money and, depending on the "job-satisfaction," grow to like it—or do not need to work but find a longing to express themselves?

The point at issue is whether Victorian women were at last getting opportunities and, if so, had they always wanted them? To return to Henrietta of *The Way we Live Now*, she may not be attracted by nursing but she obviously prefers it as somewhat more ennobling than a loveless marriage. Her wits were quick, her reading deep, and it was less the social deprivation of the post she suggests than the paucity of self-enlightenment. "If you won't take me away with you when you go away with Felix, I must stay behind and try and earn my bread. I suppose I could go out as a nurse" (chapter 84). No disrespect to Florence Nightingale is involved as she obviously saw herself as some sort of "companion" with first-aid additions!

We now turn to that category called "blue-stocking." Dickens obviously feels that the women who go to the "Philosophy and Humanity" lectures do so to the detriment of their housewifely duties. In *Martin Chuzzlewit*, Mr. Bevan informed the hero that "ordinary domestic drudgery was far below the range of these Philosophers" (chapter 17).

We may bridle here and wonder why they should care about "drudgery," but in the same sentence we read that this means that not one of the group can do "the easiest woman's work for herself'—obviously we are not only having Dickens's frequent sarcasm about Americans but also the implications that anything in a house was drudgery! In *Our Village*, Emily sounds sensibly educated, yet Miss Mitford conveys that she only gets away with this by the addition of charm, "Carefully—conducted education, acting on a mind of singular clearness and ductility matured and improved by the very best company," but one never thinks of her acquirements.

It is the charming artless character, the bewitching sweetness of manner, the real and universal sympathy—that one loves in Emily. ("The Old House at Aberleigh"). Emily herself is not hiding any "blue-stocking" tendencies and Miss Mitford has said earlier that she is clever almost as one of Shakespeare's heroines: it just wouldn't be deemed *comme il faut* in Miss Mitford's eyes to have a heroine who thrust her knowledge at anyone! In *Rhoda Fleming*, Edmund writes: "All here take an interest in parliamentary affairs. They can talk to men on men's themes. It is impossible to explain to you how wearisome an everlasting nursery prattle becomes." This is to explain to Dahlia how she should occupy herself in London lodgings (chapter 22). In the same chapter, Meredith remarks that "there is a democratic virus secret in every woman—the rights of individual manhood were likely to be recognised—in defiance of station, of reason, of all those ideas inculcated by education and society." In other words, both Edmund and Meredith liked women to have a bit of get up and go, but the blue-stocking possibility had been ignored in first seducing Dahlia and then expecting her to act like an educated wife even though not elevated to that status!

In Disraeli's *Sybil*, the younger Lady Marnay is described as having "No inconsiderable talents and an intelligence richly cultivated—"but the controversial genius of her husband had completely cowed her conversational charms." This is not because he resents a clever wife but because he does not wish to be contradicted no matter how pleasantly. Men also exacerbated his nerves or temper if they took the opposite standpoint from himself.

In *Wives and Daughters*, women may be exceedingly well-educated and of lively mind, but this was not in any way to be thrust upon men, although they know men who frequently forced their views on others. We are not returning to my earlier subject of what "caught" a husband but stressing that it just wasn't a nice thing either in front of your female or your male friends to even approach the appearance or instincts of a "blue-stocking" (whether or not the phrase ever crossed their minds). "She taught Molly to read and write but tried honestly to keep her back in every other branch of education. It was only by fighting and struggling hard that, bit by bit, Molly persuaded her father to let her have French and drawing lessons. He was always afraid of her becoming too much educated—"! This is from a very well-educated country doctor (the lady in question being her governess) who has "an unusually good library," which Molly is to ransack in any case. He locked the medical books in his surgery but must have known that Molly read every other book in that library, even if she took refuge in the branches of a cherry-tree to do so! (chapter 3).

Mrs. Kirkpatrick, Molly's future stepmother, is only tolerated among the great ladies at Cumnor House on drawing-room terms (she was first employed as a governess when the girls were younger) if "the subjects spoken about did not refer to serious solid literature, or science, or politics or social economy. About novels, poetry, travels and gossip, personal details or anecdotes of any kind, she always made exactly the remarks which are expected from an agreeable listener." Yet Lady Cumnor prided herself on her position in society and her Lord Holling-ford, her son, was such that his "scientific acquirements were consider-able enough to entitle him to much reputation in the European republic of learned men" (chapters 3, 4). Nor do we notice his mother awed in conversation with him. Obviously it would just be boring and distasteful if a woman "aerated" on these subjects!

Mr. Phillotson in *Jude the Obscure* regards Sue's intellect as far sharper than his own. "Her intellect sparkles like diamonds, while mine smoulders like brown paper." He has been her teacher in some fields of intellect and saw her mind at close quarters, so no doubt was able to assess the situation adroitly and, feeling as he does about her emotion-ally, can forget male chauvinism. Moreover, on the principle that "noth-ing succeeds like success," Sue has been to a Training College, which had not been the opportunity of young ladies in other novels mentioned in this chapter. And yet Hardy himself is to point out that not all girls at the college were to benefit from the training "—amid the storms and strains of after years, with their injustice, loneliness, child-bearing, and bereavement, their minds would revert to this experience as to some-thing which had been allowed to slip past them insufficiently regarded" (chapter 3, Part 3).

Sue herself saw the college as a means to an end as she told Jude, "I will pass rather high, I expect and Mr. Phillotson will use his influence to get me a big School." To be a first-grade teacher, it has become necessary to obtain a bit of paper, but Sue was doing very well before. What of the other poor girls whom Hardy feels doomed by biology alone to make little use even of a poor training? He speaks mysteriously of their being branded the "Weaker Sex" and that "—no exertion of their own could make them strong while the inexorable laws of nature remain what they are." Presumably Sue is breaking these laws in her future conduct so gets what is coming to her! That the male sex might change its attitude a little might have seemed more feasible than waiting for

'Nature' to change? Hardy manages it in admiring Sue, why assume
other men might not also come to do so?

Caroline Stanhope in *Barchester Towers* is very intelligent and an
exceedingly good conversationalist, but Trollope implies this is not "a
good thing" as she uses her gifts to show total indifference to religion,
although her father is a high dignitary of the Church. "She prided
herself on her total freedom from English prejudice, and she might
have added, from feminine delicacy" (chapter 9). As Dr. Stanhope had
been absent in Italy for many years, his own religious faith was pretty
tenuous, but because he is a man, his bon-vivant tendencies are overlooked. It is the same with Becky Sharp. "She has a hard nature, we
know, exacerbated by a very hard childhood leading to a tendency to
look after number one." However, she is witty and considering she is
self-educated, extremely good material for higher education. Thackeray
obviously admires more than his Amelia, if one is to judge by the loving
trouble he takes to make her come alive for us. Yet, never does he
suggest that a better Society would have given Becky's wits higher opportunities. She might have been a shyster, whatever her profession, but
there are plenty of them in both sexes! "All the ladies in Paris voted her
charming. She spoke their language admirably. She adopted at once
their grace, their liveliness, their manner" (chapter 34). In England, her
"wit, flippancy and cleverness made her speedily the vogue in London
among a certain class (chapter 37). It turns out that this class numbers
the aristocracy and the dandies "among its ranks but ladies of any virtue
hesitate." Yet, basically, it need never have come to all this because in
the beginning we hear her father's conversation "was a thousand times
more agreeable to her than the talk of such of her own sex as she had
now encountered." What is more, she "had not been much of a dissem-
bler, until now her loneliness had taught her to feign" (chapter 1). Miss
Pinkerton's Establishment and her father's rogue tendencies had much
to answer for, each in their own way. Purity, beauty and charm will
attract the male eye before they notice as does Egremont with
Sybil—"the earnestness of her intellect as remarkable as the almost sa-
cred repose of her mien and manner."

Disraeli at least gives us a hero who is struck by strength of intellect,
but Thackeray seems to think intellect may be easily a tool for evil and
Hardy that it may be an instrument of suffering. The Dean's daughter
in *Barchester Towers* is described as "Very learned in stones, ferns, plants
and vermin and had written a book about petals." We also read that

"She was a wonderful woman in her way." But Trollope implies that her way is very spinsterish. Even her name, Miss Trefoil, mocks her main preoccupation and we meet her first at Mrs. Proudie's party literally being a "support" to her father as he totters in on her arm. No doubt being a general support to him was Society's view of her main role in life although her botany was probably of greater interest to her had she "told all"!

In *Cranford*, Mrs. Gaskell speaks of what is known as "A solid English education." 'Fancy-work and the use of the globes—such as the mistress of the 'Ladies' Seminary professed to teach." Certainly Miss Matty went to school before Queen Victoria was on the throne, but the girl who tells the story, speaking for Mrs. Gaskell, is well aware that now Miss Matty is down on her luck and they are reviewing ways of earning a living for her. Teaching would hardly be suitable for her abilities much as it would suit her to be "Thrown among the little elves in whom her soul delighted" (chapter 14). In other words Mrs. Gaskell recognises that women's Education is slowly advancing and rightly so. The critic Marjorie Bald, in *Women Writers in the Nineteenth Century*, feels that Mrs. Gaskell may admire intelligence in women (especially in real life, as with Emily and Charlotte Bronte) but that she puts "Womenly characteristics first i.e., a housewifely disposition" and "A delicate neatness" next and perhaps, above all, "a restful presence"—instancing that Molly Gibson is thought of by her father as "—a peacemaker and a sweetener of intercourse." Marjorie Bald also points out that Cousin Phyllis loves Latin." She reads it in the evening that she may enjoy it the more." Yet Mrs. Gaskell is to remark that she can enjoy what the critic sums up as "A simple round of homely pleasure" and is thereby (in her creator's eye) the more cultured in a true sense." How Mrs. Gaskell defines culture here is open to speculation.

However, other women authors have a more practical approach. The Brontes, having had to earn their own livings and not particularly enjoying it, see that love of one's subject or, at least pleasanter working conditions, might motivate other women to fuller lives. In *The Tenant of Wildfell Hall*, Helen paints with skill and is not ashamed to sell her pictures for money, remarking to Markham, "Perhaps few people gain their livelihood with so much pleasure in their task as I do" (chapter 9). Circumstances have changed Helen from a frivolous girl to a separated wife with an urgent need to keep her son. No doubt this would make earning one's living more "respectable" to the Victorian, but one is sure Anne Bronte did not view things this way.

In *The Professor*, once Frances has overcome her discipline problems and is teaching subjects she enjoys, at a better type of school, her profession means so much to her that when Crimsworth proposes, she states, "I should like of course to retain my employment—my efforts to get on will be as unrestrained as yours." Crimsworth, doing the manly thing, tells the reader that a man should provide for those he loves and tells Frances she must rest and that her salary will not add much to their income. Despite Frances's gentle manner and her tendency still to call him "Master," she answers firmly, "Think of my marrying to be kept by you! I could not do it. And think how dull my days would be" (chapter 23). Hurray! Frances has often seemed rather "wet" in her attitudes, but here speaks the modern woman. There is no point going into the fact that sheer laziness, genuine love of housewifely tasks, limited parental outlook, may lead women of the 1980s to feel exactly the opposite, but the voice of the woman that one *can* be speaks here. Apart from teaching and artistic expression, business ability can evince itself under stress. To turn to a male writer for a moment, Marie Melmotte may have "been only a child" when her father put money in her name, but when he demands it back, she sees straight through his claim that it should be liable to the ordinary fluctuations of "commercial enterprise," retorting sharply, "So that nobody should get at it," adding later "But it is mine!." She is not attempting to cheat him, by her own standards, but is fighting for her independence and thus her intelligence is sharpened (Trollope: *The Way We Live Now*, chapter 78).

In all, we find that certain men are to value brains, especially if already bored by beauty (long before Crimsworth meets Frances, he refers to the tedium of "carmine lips—that will soon fade if there is no Promethean spark of intellect" (*Professor*, chapter 1). Likewise, we find women who are pining to use their intellect, regardless of whether men are interested or not. Nevertheless, although women authors show more, naturally, of this longing in their heroines than men authors unless these heroines are established spinsters, a hero is somehow anticipated as being a complementary necessity to these girls "one day." For example, Shirley, a "fiery free speaker," as we will see in a later chapter, seeks a mate who will appreciate her freedom-need. Fair enough, one might say, but should this be the only true expression of her spirit?

Education has always been a social process by means of which the society involved has sought to transmit to the emergent generation those aspects of its culture that are considered fundamental and vital for its stability and survival. English education in the nineteenth century was less consciously nationalistic than that in European countries but, it is generally admitted, it was deeply influenced by social class structure.

Formal education can be a component of social change. It can also be an obstruction to change. Socially, a system of education needs to imprint attitudes that are going to be important rather than attitudes that have been important. The planning of education is an exercise in social eugenics and demands maximum appreciation of social and cultural trends. Schools and colleges are major agencies of cultural preservation, transmission, and potential progress. Schools reflect the orientation of the society as a whole. The citizen who lacks education is bound to be the slave of others.

The first teachers were priests who knew about the traditions and customs of their societies and thus the first schools were in religious meeting places. In the nineteen century, there were many small private schools in England, but they were very inefficient, often being kept by unqualified teachers. One of these schools was described in a report to the Education Committee in Liverpool in 1836 as a place "in the compass of 10 feet by 9 inches in which forty children were taught. "On a perch forming a triangle with the corner of the room sat a cock and two hens. There was only one small window at which sat the master."

The functionalist perspective on education laid the main emphasis on teaching religion and morality. The primary objective for the education of the labouring poor was to "gentle the masses" and to inculcate religion and morals so that children and students would "submit to the higher powers." In 1822 a philanthropic society, supporting education, argued that a moral and religious education should be provided for the whole of the poor.

In nineteenth-century England, elementary education was provided by voluntary organisations. The state did not begin to participate in the support of education until 1833 when Parliamant made its first grant for education. It was not until 1870 that the Education Act was passed, permitting the election of school boards and the levy of local taxes to provide elementary schools in addition to those maintained by the voluntary societies. This act did not make any provisions for secondary education, which was conducted by voluntary fees. England did not develop a system of publicly supported secondary education schools until after 1902. The provision of education for girls had to wait the end of the century.

Secondary education in nineteenth-century England meant largely the old public schools and their new imitators. The education they offered was criticised by many writers and teachers. H. Sidgwick, an eminent educationalist, criticised the neglect of English language and literature and omission of science from the public school curriculum. "I think," he wrote, "a course of instruction in our language and literature and a course of instruction in natural science ought to form recognised and substantive parts of our school system." In the early years of the nineteenth century, the public schools were corrupt and very inefficient. Reform of these schools was undertaken by teachers who might be described as "classical humanists." They, including Matthew Arnold, were anxious to remove the corruption and incompetence and to establish a liberal education with the emphasis on classics as the main vehicle for education. The whole system of university education reflected the way of life of the eighteenth-century aristocracy and squirearchy rather than scholarship.

All social and cultural structures in nineteenth-century England were male-dominated. It is not, therefore, surprising that there was hardly any provision of education for girls. Like their mothers, they were treated by class-driven and egoistic utilitarian society as "weaker sex," doomed by "inferior genetic endowment" to serve their male partners. Most male writers supported this biological prejudice in order to maintain their gender supremacy.

In France, some writers, including Rousseau, were pleased that there were no colleges for girls. Similarly, in England, some male writers, including Thomas Hardy, believed in the inferiority of the female sex, indicating that "there is no point in educating girls." By contrast, all female writers, including the Brontes, Elizabeth E. Gaskell, and George Eliot, dismissed the pseudo-biological conception of sex and correctly argued that women and girls are not only not inferior to men and boys but are in many respect intellectually superior to them.

The proposition of Enlightenment philosophy that the soul or spirit has no sex did not attract male writers who blindly adhered to the view that the male sex supremacy is genetically determined. The philosophy of liberal radicalism contained many elements of Spencerian evolutionism, resting on the principle of the survival of the bodily fittest.

With the exception of J. S. Mill, the utilitarians showed no interest either in equality or in rights. In their egoistic strivings, their principal concern was with self-interest—with utility. There was no sympathetic feeling for the subjugated female in male-dominated society.

In the second half of the nineteenth-century, there was, however, a general awakening of social conscience, which led to the provision of education for girls. Following the establishment of the Girls' Public School in 1872, London University opened its degree examinations for women in 1878. J. S. Mill's campaign for women's suffrage in the sixties and seventies, supported by Francis Nightingale, prepared the way for the founding of women's colleges and the improvement of girls's schools.

# CHAPTER 4

# LOVE AND MARRIAGE AND PLATONIC FRIENDSHIP

Many and varied are the attitudes of women to marriage, but those of men, at least among the pages of the nineteenth-century literature, seems to vary only between the smug and the unrealistically idealistic. This, at least, is how women writers and the more ironic male writers see it. When Dorothea waxes enthusiastically about how she sees her future role as Casaubon's wife, he is very touched, but, nevertheless, "He was not surprised (what lover would have been?) that he should have been the object of it"! That Dorothea is not being really true to her ultimate self here is brought out in the next chapter when we read that she has no coyness with Sir James Chettam once he accepts that she doesn't love him. "She was perfectly unconstrained and without irritation towards him now, and he was discovering the frank kindness and companionship between a man and a woman who have no passion to hide or confess" (*Middlemarch*: chapters 5 and 8).

Dorothea is an unusual heroine, but although her enthusiastic plans for an intellectual future with Casaubon blind her to the lack of any real love on her side, she is not at all puzzled by his inordinate vanity in receiving her raptures so mildly. Men's right to expect devotion was an "accepted thing," evidently, in her mind—whereas the cessation of enthusiasm on Sir James's side was a refreshing change. He was relieved, when he got used to his rejection, but the pleasures of platonic friendship must also have brought relief to her fervid mind alike.

The sad reality of Victorian marriage—and alas of some marriages today—is occasionally spotted, although not sufficiently deplored by a loving parent. Caleb Garth, talking to Mary about Fred, remarks sadly: "A woman, let her be as good as she may, has got to put up with the life her husband makes for her. Your mother has had to put up with a great deal because of me" (*Middlemarch*, chapter 25). Mary is sensible enough to know for herself that Fred is not ready for marriage yet, whatever his feelings, and being a working girl, does not see marriage as an end in itself. The case of Edith Wharton in *The Prime Minister* is a much sadder one. We hear she is an intelligent, spirited girl, but Trollope drily observes "A girl can look forward to little else than the chance of a good husband: a good man, or if her tastes lie in that direction, a rich man." Men, we have just heard, have endless other things to look forward to and "Marriage, if it comes is just an accident—" (P.M. chapter 5).

Charlotte Bronte's *Shirley*, as we would expect, is very frank about marriage to Caroline. "To tell you a secret, if *I* were convinced that they are necessarily different from us—fickle, soon petrifying, unsympathising—I should never marry" (chapter 12). The nature of the opposite ·sex is what concerns Shirley and who is to blame her? Marriage is not so inevitable to her mainly because she has money and many interests. She still feels, however, that marriage is a part of her future and shocks Caroline by adding "That discovery once made, what should I long for? To go away—to remove from a presence where my society gave no pleasure" i.e., if husband should prove indifferent (chapter 12).

In fact, by the end of the conversation, they have decided that marriage is a very dicey business altogether: but no thought of changing the rules of the game! Caroline is already committed in that she already loves Robert Moore and when she thinks, later, that Shirley loves him too, she speaks strongly to her heart, as Charlotte's heroines tend to do: "Let them be married then: but afterwards I shall be nothing to him. As for being his sister, and all that stuff, I despise it. I will either be all or nothing to a man like Robert; no feeble shuffling or false cant is endurable" (chapter 14). The strange convention by which it is somehow unladylike or unwomanly or both to admit, even to oneself, of loving a man before he declares himself is not met here—presumably because her mother hasn't been part of her formative years or because sensible Northern blood does not follow the tradition. Helen's aunt in *The Tenant of Wildfell Hall* states almost as a dogma, "It is not to be supposed that you would wish to marry anyone till you were asked; a girl's affections should never be won unsought" (Anne Bronte: *Tenant of Wildfell Hall*, chapter 16).

Helen's aunt listens to her niece's assurances that she could never give her heart before giving firm approval of a man's character, i.e., respect for him and wisely warns that an impetuous girl of eighteen is likely to fall in love with the first handsome flatterer. Helen promptly does this but with hindsight is still to say to Markham that such advice "May be as good as far as it went—but there are some things she has overlooked. I wonder if she was ever in love." Her aunt appeared happily married, so presumably thoughtless young love was being referred to. At least Aunt is not "matchmaking" and is anxious Helen should marry for the right reasons even if love is not one of the main ingredients. The mother of her friend, Milicent Hargrave, is totally ruthless. Milicent writes to Helen: "I should not care if I could see any prospect of being able to love and admire him, but I can't. There is nothing about him to hang one's esteem and affection upon; he is diametrically opposite to what I imagined my husband should be." (*The Tenant of Wildfell Hall*, chapter 25).

At the end of the chapter, we read "Poor Milicent, I fear, had fallen a sacrifice to the manoeuvrings of this mistaken mother, who congratulates herself on having so satisfactorily discharged her maternal duty—". This mother has made financial sacrifices for her son and has thus made her daughters "portionless," incidentally. Showing off her girls to the world, she wanted a "better chance" for them: so, in fact, marriage was a type of career, which was to take the place of her boy's profession! Thackeray confounds the theory that "marriages of convenience" can grow into love in *The Virginians* when Fannay says to the Countess of Castlewood, "I am sure you married our papa without liking him. You have told me a thousand times!" And her brother takes this up with, "If you did not like him before marriage you certainly did not love him afterwards. Fan & I remember how our beloved parents used to fight. Don't us, Fan?" (Part 1, chapter 17). Thackeray is parodying certain upper-class mores and those of an earlier century, but Sue Bridehead, speaking at the end of the nineteenth century, states, "Fewer women like marriage than you suppose. They only enter it for the dignity it is assumed to confer, and the social advantages it gains them sometimes—a dignity and advantage. I am well able to do without" (Part 5, chapter 1). Later, as they watch a wedding, she says to Jude "The flowers in the bride's hand are sadly like the garland which decked the heifers of sacrifice in the old times." Constriction and coercion seem to be on her mind, though she is speaking to Jude, whom she loves and who retorts that men often feel the same pressures. In other words, though theirs would not be a marriage without love, Sue still feels it is "of convenience" because they are considering it for the child's sake. Even though Dickens makes Merry seem farcical before she marries, we know from her later sufferings that he speaks solemnly through the lips of Mr. Chuzzlewit who says, "Remember from your bridal hour to the day you are brought as low as these" (pointing to some graves) "there will be no appeal against him" (chapter 24).

To turn aside for a moment from what made women marry and what could be the result, let us return to why they fell in love in the first place. "Manhood" is a quality much admired by some women in Victorian Literature. Gertrude did not regret her choice of Alaric as a husband, even when he was disgraced and Harry had inherited Normans-grove (Trollope: *The Three Clerks* chapter 63). Trollope gives an interesting analysis of what this "manhood" consists because apparently had all Harry's "virtues been bright as burnished gold," they would not have outweighed Aleric's special quality. Sporting ability was important, but that was not quite all; good breeding, which Harry also possessed, but perhaps flaunted less? Whatever it was, Gertrude made a kind of Knights of Old thing about it and when Aleric was disgraced, she sticks by him, although of a very proud nature herself. "Such is the love of which a man is *not* capable" (chapter 38).

By the time we come to an equally fastidious but more thoughtful young lady in Hardy's *A Laodicean*, we see that Paula, partly through circumstances, partly through social developments, is able to say, "In matrimony as in some other things you should be slow to decide; but quick to execute. Nothing on earth would make me marry another man. I know every fibre of his being and he knows a good many fibres of mine, so, as there is no more to be learnt, why shouldn't we marry at once?" (Part 6, chapter 3). Esther gradually comes to appreciate Felix Holt because of his abilities and his sacrifices for the people he believes in." He has chosen an intolerable life; though I suppose if I had a mind like his, and he loved me dearly, I should choose the same life" (George Eliot, *Felix Holt*, chapter 22). Her later thoughts on the difference between her two suitors, Harold and Felix, are very perceptive. We may laugh at her desire to be subjugated; it is also based on a desire of being married to an inferior, if flattering man. She recalls that she once said to Felix, "A woman must choose meaner things because mean things are offered to her" (chapter 43).

In *The Hand of Ethelberta*, the heroine expresses the opinion that half the pain of love is that a woman's form and opinion of her choice before she has half seen him and loved him before she has half formed an opinion" (chapter 19). A wry thought, equally applicable today, but fewer chances then of seeing a man enough among other men in natural surroundings. Then again there is the fact that a woman falls in love with a man just because she can't help it—as often expressed in novels and in real life, today! Hesther in *Sylvia's Lovers* imagines that just because she loves Phillip so much all would have been smooth if she had been married to him. Mrs. Gaskell comments drily, "The resisting forces that make all such harmony and delight impossible are not recognised by the bystanders, hardly by the actors" (chapter 35). In other words no matter what little chance you seem to have gaining the other person's affections, one still feels there is something about him that conjures up the thought of bliss in connection with the future shared with him. To return to Ethelberta for a moment, she tells Picotee that there is a middle state between loving and not loving when one can draw back "At the beginning of caring for a man—just when you are suspended between thought and feeling—there is a hairbreadth of time at which the question of getting into love or not getting in is a matter of will—quite a matter of choice." The sad thing about his advice to her sister is that Picotee loves someone who has in the past loved Ethelberta and is soon to love her again. While Ethelberta's advice is based on the fact that the rich would not want to marry either of them—so one must hesitate before falling in love, a poor man might well be irritated by such hesitations. Thus class and man's dominant role in courtship rule what might otherwise be very wise advice (Hardy: *The Hand of Ethelberta*, chapter 6).

In marriage itself women frequently dominated in the home—though they are not necessarily depicted as very pleasant women for doing so! It was as if it was their province and domination that would keep them from poking in anywhere else or a more charitable husband might feel that women were good at "that sort of thing," so must be allowed to be boss. Rosey's mother, Mrs. Kackenzie, is an extreme example in *The Newcomers*, but then she is the archetypal mother-in-law. "My mother-in-law cried out that I should drop the baby and only the Colonel knew how to hold it." She is even openly haughty to Colonel Newcome's new business connections and in-laws, but on being told she can move elsewhere, if she does not like the company, she refrains. Although "she abstained from overt hostilities against any guests—she contended herself with assuming grand and princessly airs in the company of the new ladies" (chapters 69 and 70). Sweet and loving wives did not insist on a point, if it was not directly connected with house-keeping. "There, now, you are angry and we won't talk of it any more." To this Widere maddeningly answers, "That is how you always back out. She is the stronger character by far but the accepted thing for a good wife was to create harmony." Impossible here, of course, as they were an incompatible pair (chapter 6, book 5). The Duchess of Omnium is very harsh and outspoken to her husband, if it was for his best interests. "It was her nature to say such things—and he knew they came from her uncontrolled spirit rather than any malice." And "She was essentially one of those women who are not contented to be known as the wives of their husbands" (chapter 6).

On the subject of Platonic friendship, it is interesting to have a man's opinion for a moment, if only to analyse whether women were much given to pining for the same thing. In *Diana of the Crossways*, Dacier reflects: "She was a pleasant friend; just a soft bit sweeter than male friends which gave the flavour of sex without the artful seduction" (chapter 19). A little earlier, he thinks over the rumours about her affair with his uncle and decides to discount them and take the true version. "At any rate she was capable of friendship. Why not resolutely believe that she had been his uncle's true and simple friend!"

Ethelberta herself wishes that there could be "Warm friendship between herself and him (Ladywell) as well as all her other lovers, without that insistent courtship and marriage business that sent them all scattering like leaves in a pestilential blast, at enmity with one another" (chapter 35). Of course Ethelberta's character is not so genuinely independent as Diana's (Hardy and Meredith looking for different things in their heroines!), but nevertheless she goes about reading her poetry risking the acrimony of her own sex who, we read, consider that "To move about unchaperoned—society grants only to the famous, the ministering, and the improper"! Ethelberta enjoys this freedom of movement and expects that ordinary friendship with men should follow. Her manner was probably too unconsciously flirtatious to make this possible, but still the desire was there.

Madame La Duchess D'Ivry considers it quite suitable to have a platonic friendship with a young grazier of an aspiring mind and remarkable poetic talents, thereby disregarding the fact that "His pretty young wife was rendered miserable by all these readings but what could a poor little country-woman know of Platonism" (Thackeray: *Newcomes*, chapter 36). This was of course appalling snobbery both social and intellectual, but that it was platonic there could be no doubt as both the man and the woman communicated solely on the poetic plane. Lucy Roberts believes in "an ordinary, comfortable masculine friendship," although after conversation with her sister-in-law, she realises that more "feelings" are involved on her side and more "attentions" on Lord Lufton's than she had realised. This does not detract from the fact that there was less coyness in her manner and more bonhommie in his than we expect of the Victorian maiden. (*Framley Parsonage,* chapter 13). We saw under "Sexual Equality" that Lord Lufton is all for women being free to go unchaperoned about the world and to earn their livings. The fact that the couple fall in love does not mean that their friendship was not genuinely platonic in the first place. Older women, rich women, slightly risqué women: all these could seek platonic friendship without risking ridicule. But only as the Victorian era progressed would men, scheming or genuinely anxious mothers see anything but matrimony on the horizon for young, innocent girls, and the latter had to have a great deal of spirit to wish for anything else.

# CHAPTER 5

# PROSTITUTION AND ILLEGITIMACY

At first glance these two subjects may seem an unnecessary conjunction, but I place them together as there was the same hush-hush attitude in polite society and the same tender sympathy among individuals of all classes towards both topics.

Lord Kew speaks harshly of Barnes Newcome, telling us of a poor girl "whom he brought out of a Newcome factory when he was a boy himself—whom he ill-treated, whom he flung out of doors without a penny—who came and sat down on the very steps of Park Lane with a child on each side of her and not their cries nor their hunger but—the dread of a police-court forced him to give her a maintenance" (*Newcomes*, Part 1, chapter 33). Admittedly, Kew then softens this story but only by saying he had heard that Barnes suggested a school in Yorkshire, but she did not want to part with them (recalling Nicholas Nickleby, no one will be surprised!)

When one turns to Mrs. Gaskell's *Ruth*, one naturally expects a more tender approach both from a woman writer and a minister's wife, who saw much suffering at first hand. Yet her attitude is tempered always by the thought that although the seductions of young men must be blamed, the foolishness of young women has to be stressed as the "morals" of the young lady reader must be protected.

All this said, there is something new and solemn in the words of Thurstan Benson: "She has incurred a responsibility—I fancy such responsibility must be solemn enough, without making it into a heavy and serious burden, so that human nature recoils from bearing it" (chapter 11). Miss Benson is a little dry and sarcastic in answer and yet cooperates in giving Ruth a home. It is Miss Benson who has to reason with her brother, years later, against the wisdom of letting Ruth work for the Bradshaws. "Have we any right to ruin her prospects for life by telling Mr. Bradshaw all we know of her errors? Only sixteen when she did so wrong, and never to escape from it all in her years to come—to have the despair of it being known clutching her back into worse sin? What harm do you think she can do? What is the risk to which you are exposing Mr. Bradshaw's family?" (chapter 18). Ruth is an interesting study from other points of view. Losing her mother young, she is not told the facts of life." She was too young when her mother died to have received cautious words of advice respecting the subject of a woman's life" (chapter 3). Moreover, when she is seduced, she seems to need the prod of scandal before she fully realises her complete loss of social caste. When Harry, a little boy in Wales, punches her in the face because he has somehow overheard she is "naughty," she then realises that far from just being "happy" with Bellingham, she is considered as "wrong" for living with someone who is not married to her. Ruth, in fact, feels married to someone she worships without questioning; it is only the advent of the baby that totally changes things.

As regards actual streetwalkers, the M.P. Rainer has evidently a tender heart because he speaks of "Keeping silver in his pocket for poor girls on their way home" and of rescuing a suicide attempt by a girl who was using the jump as "A last philosophy" (*Diana of the Crossways*, chapter 17). He is offhand about it in chatting to Redworth, because obviously it would have been more fashionable to use their services, but, sardonic or not, the intimations are there from Meredith that the girls are to be pitied. The "kept woman" is referred to by men in a slightly different way. Caterina is not a prostitute in the ordinary sense, but "The World" imagines her to have been won at dice from Lord March whereas the innocent Henry Warrington thinks of her as a pure ballet dancer. When her mother enquires why he did not "take pay for the services he had rendered the young person" (i.e., the jewels and so on she had persuaded him to buy her), he cries out, "He came from a country where the very savages would recoil from such a bargain" and expresses horror that she should "Traffic in her daughter's dishonour." (*Virginians*, Part 1, chapter 11).

Whether savages would recoil is another story. The fact remains that Harry and Thackeray apparently do. Another attitude of interest is Lord Loughborough's attitude to little Annabella, who is presumably the child of Arthur or the man Lady Loughborough escaped with to the Continent (*Tenant of Wildfell Hall*, chapter 50). "He had obliged himself to treat her with paternal kindness, he had forced himself not to hate her, and even perhaps to feel some degree of kindly regard for

her in return for her artless and unsuspecting attachment to himself."
So, he doesn't condemn the child in any way and struggles desperately
against strong feelings of a wish to hate her, but he still thinks of her as
"an innocent being": A change from many of the condemnatory ladies
we have heard from in other novels. Here I say ladies, rather than
"women" as we saw more tolerance among the poor. In "A Few Crusted
Characters," the women in the carrier's cart listening to the tale of
"Andy Satchel and the Parson" are not horrified that Jane "has" to get
married, because in the thatcher's words "Of the bodily circumstances
owing to that young man"; instead they cry out, "Ah! poor thing!" sym-
pathising with her without any hint of censure.

On the other hand, this may merely reveal Hardy's insight into
rustic ways, because Miggs in *Barnaby Rudge* shows great spite and
malice: "To such as had been frail—she showed no mercy." Dickens
does not, of course, admire this trait, hinting that because of her plain-
ness, spinsterhood and pseudo-evangelical tendencies, she is equally inflexible and grim to anyone who could establish any claim to beauty."

Another slant on this subject—and one that bears thinking about
in our own century is Trollope's delicately worded suggestion that the
woman who marries for money is little better than "the wretch who
earns her bread in the lowest stage of degradation" (*Framley Parsonage*,
chapter 21). Trollope pursues this line again with Lizzie Eustache. "She
may not have sacrificed her beauty to a lover—she has never sacrificed
anything to anybody." (*Eustace Diamonds*, chapter 9).

In John McVeagh's Introduction to *Ruth*, he speaks of Mrs. Gaskell
"diminishing by a perceptible margin one of society's meanest injustices
to women" and later he speaks of Ruth coming to see herself as a person
and less as a permanently damaged "reputation". In *Mary Barton*, Jem
Wilson turns from a prostitute until he recognises Esther as a definite
person—then he "Took her hand and shook it with a cordiality that
forgot the present in the past" (chapter 14). Esther then relates how she
took to the streets, and we once again pick up the thread of illegitimacy.
"My child was ill, so ill, and I was starving. And I could not bear to see
her suffer—so I went out into the street one January night. Do you think
God will punish me for that?" Is chapter 21 the reader is told that when
Mary is speaking to her aunt, "No faint imagination of the love and woe
of that poor creature crossed her mind or she would have taken her, all
guilty and erring to her bosom and tried to bind up that broken heart."

Miss Wade's story in *Little Dorrit* concerns the stigma of illegitimacy, but yet the sister of her employer's husband was also "born out of wedlock" and "much loved and cherished" (Dickens: *Little Dorrit*, chapter 21). Thus we see that "Society's views counted for little if the persons closest to the case were tender and loving." The lady whom Miss Wade sarcastically calls throughout the chapter "My Mistress," although her employer seems to treat her with great tenderness and compassion, remarks, "We have been apprehensive that you may allow some family circumstances of which no one can be more innocent than yourself, prey upon your spirits. If so, let us entreat you not to make them a cause of grief. My husband, himself, as is well known, formerly had a very dear sister, who was not in law his sister, but who was universally loved and respected." How different this from Miss Barbary's appalling attitude towards Esther in *Bleak House*. But then, Miss Barbary was governed not only by a fanatical religious fervour, but by an arrogant family pride, which in the end always amounts to self-love. Miss Wade is not impressed by the tenderness of manner because, as can be seen in chapter 28, she is obsessed by "No Name" and seeks to stress to Tattycoram that her employers knew she is illegitimate but fondled and petted her because her adopters have money. "What your broken plaything is as to birth, I am. She has no name, I have no name. Her wrong is my wrong." She argues that all real affection goes to their daughter who is spoilt and childish (in Miss Wade's eyes) and will soon tire of her little maid—so the whole thing is a ludicrous patronage. Miss Wade is, in fact, wrong here as the Meagles' motives are perfectly pure, but she herself has suffered so much from condescension that one can understand that she trusts no one. When Q.D. Leavis was making enquiries into the whole question of how an illigitimate person felt, she quotes a newspaper enquiry into how people living still remembered their Victorian youth. "I have been in social work for twenty years, I am illegitimate—I have noticed one point above all: whatever their background or experience, illegitimates seem to feel the need to apologise for their existence—" (*Dickens the Novelist*, chapter 3, footnote 18).

Ambivalence reigns in the realm of general morality and I will be devoting a chapter to the subject, but, in passing, it is pleasant to remark that women always tend, if at all compassionate, to "understand." The boatman's wife, wrongly of course, half-suspects that Mary Barton is a prostitute but still remarks, "It's the sinful that have to bear the bitter, bitter grief" (chapter 31). More expectedly, as family loyalty is involved,

Rhoda Fleming goes and stands besides Dahlia when her father (normally a kind man) speaks a word that "stains her cheeks" and this, to us, natural conduct on Rhoda's part, leads to a week "of severe silence" (chapter 2). To return to Little Dorrit, she is met by a prostitute one night who rebukes poor mad Maggie for taking such a delicate child out at night. Still thinking little Dorrit is a child, she asks her for a kiss—when she then sees her face, she cowers away and implies that no innocent woman must even kiss her. Poor little Dorrit can only ask her to pretend she is a child, but the sad creature flees from her with a wild cry. The total innocense, based on ignorance, could not be "spotted" evidently, but little Dorrit's kindly heart could not surmount in the prostitute's eyes her "knowledge."

Until 40 to 50 years ago, illegitimacy or "bastardy" was regarded as a disgrace both for mother and child. This state of affairs has been gradually remedied—at least in legal systems—and today the rights of an illegitimate child are almost the same as the rights of the legitimate.

Many famous people have been born illegitimate. Charlemagne, emperor of the Holy Roman Empire, had no less than four wives and four mistresses; all the latter bore him illegitimate children. "Philip the Bastard" in Shakespeare's play *King John* was suspected to be the illegitimate son of king Richard Coeur de Lion. Don Juan of Austria, who defeated the Turks in the battle of Lepanto in 1571, was the bastard son of the Hapsburg Emperor Charles V.

Until comparatively recent times, the social and legal disabilities of an illegitimate child were considerable. He or she was "nobody's child" since the child had no lawful and often no known father. Socially, therefore, such a child lived under a stigma, which made it a kind of second-class citizen.

The sufferings of such a child have been graphically described by Charles Dickens in the person of Oliver Twist and Esther Summerson in *Bleak House*. Puritans and narrow-minded men and women tended to impute to the child the "sin" of his or her mother. Traces of this belief still exist.

In most legal systems, it is always certain who is a child's mother. The case of the father is frequently problematic. There are some wives who commit adultery and are inclined to prostitution. There are also cases in which wives have relations with a man other than the husband, and the wife may herself be uncertain who the child's father is.

It is, therefore, obvious that while maternity is easily provable, fatherhood is not. The child of a "single" woman, including one living apart from her husband at the date of birth, is generally regarded as illegitimate.

In many cases it is very difficult, if not impossible, to establish the fictitional child's fatherhood. Illegitimacy is not primarily a teenage problem. It is true that Ruth in Mrs. Gaskell's novel was only fifteen at the time of her seduction, but most illegitimate births occur to mothers aged between twenty-five and twenty-nine. The scene of Elizabeth Gaskell's married life was the grim north of the Industrial Revolution where poverty, dirt, disease, and juvenile prostitution were commonplace.

Industrialisation has contributed to the increase in the employment of women and also to the increase in illegitimacy. Since the 1870s the birth rate in most European countries has been steadily declining. By contrast, prostitution, adultery, and illegitimacy rates—due to the lack of moral values—indicate a substantial increase. This, in its turn, constitutes new social, economic, and moral problems.

# CHAPTER 6

# VICTORIAN MORALITY

Men had a certain standard, no matter how "fast" they were, if their particular class demanded it, or, alternatively, if a girl from another class had her own standards—no matter how limited. Take Ruby Ruggles for instance. She lives in a novelletish world in her imagination and would like to marry Felix Carbury for his wealth and handsome face. But the operative word is "marry." Though emotionless and ruthless, Felix knows better than to suggest she should become his mistress. "There was an animal courage about her, and an amount of strength too and a fire in her eye of which he had learned to be aware" (chapter 18). Later, living in London with her aunt, she goes secretly to a gin-palace with a "disguised" Felix and dances ecstatically, but when she finally asks him if he intends to marry her and receives a sarcastic answer, her inherent morality shows, "Not to make myself a bother! Oh, but I will, I will." When he scathingly asks her if she hasn't heard of bachelors lingering on, she trenchantly replies, "There's the Squire. But he doesn't keep asking girls to keep him company." (*The Way We Live Now*, chapter 18).

Slight double standards are here in that Ruby never stops to analyse whether any real love is in her heart for Felix, but her moral standard, as such, does not appear to be hypocritical. Women in higher society are more hypocritical in some Victorian works. Thackeray points out the very women who draw away from Lady Clara are secretly having affairs. In other words the old Eleventh Commandment, "Thou Shalt Not Be Found OUT." Barnes has driven her by his cruelty to fly to her first lover, Lord Highgate. "People as criminal but undiscovered, make room for her as if her touch were pollution" (Thackeray: *The Newcomes*, Pt. 2, chapter 63). On the other hand, thoughtful men can be very stringent to their own sex on the subject. Mr. Benson, after Ruth's death, speaks coldly to Mr. Donne, pointing out that his conduct to the girl was a great deal more than "youthful folly" (chapter 36). Donne mutters to himself when he is alone again that Benson is nothing but "An ill-bred, puritanical fellow"—thereby making the usual excuses of class and broad-mindedness for his own insensitivity!

Preventative morality rather than actual trust in their daughters sometimes seems the order of the day with mothers. Jack Lambert's wife in *The Virginians* is very trenchant regarding women as a "temptation," but, in discussing Hetty with the girl's sister Theo, she remarks, "I have every trust in Jack, of course" (her husband) "but I should like to see them come together in my house, when I'm upstairs, I promise you." This is not aimed at either party in particular. She has already remarked she has every trust in Jack—but: "He is a man. Every man is a man, with all his sanctified airs." Poor Jack, being a parson, gives rise to the adjective rather than any hypocritical manner! All this seems to be a sort of morality by default, rather than a cogent creed (*Virginians*, 86). Thackeray is of course, looking back to a century not famed for morality, but tinging his writing with an attitude suitable for the Victorian lady.

When we move a decade or so and a world away in attitude to Meredith's *The Egoist*, we read rather sadly that other women do not care for girls who are not completely innocent—even though they themselves have "lifted a veil to be seen and peeped at a world where innocence is as poor a guarantee as a babe's caul against shipwreck" (chapter 5). This perfect innocence, Meredith tells us, is part of an overlord's pride of possession and we should not blame women for lacking the courage that in the end leads to lack of conscience because men have trained them thus in seeking perfection. In other words she could not "be herself" with such a man as Willoughby. The reason for these reflections on the author's part are based on Clara's "fibs and evasions" brought about by W.'s "ridiculous standards" (chapter 25).

In a sense *The Egoist* is a Comedy of Manners; in another sense it is a very moving satire: all this depending on whether you look at Willoughby's point of view or Clara's. Meredith suggests witheringly that if the latter had been a little more frank with Willoughby, she, among other society women would "be guilty of effrontery and forfeit the waxen polish of purity and thus their position in society" (Ibid). Notice the particularly artificial nature of "waxen polish." In *Diana of the Crossways*, Emma maintains that English women are expected to be "black" or "white" and she thinks it is because "there is a fiction that their homes are purer than elsewhere" (chapter 14). She is talking to Diana of being the "fiction" in the society that they themselves were born into but adds thoughtfully "There is a class that does live honestly; at any rate it springs from a liking for purity; but I am sure their method of impressing it on their womenfolk is artificial. They narrow their understanding of human nature, and that is not the way to improve the breed." Emma is, in fact, as basically moral as the next Victorian matron, but she is perceptive and tolerant enough to see "The wife madly stripped before the world by a jealous husband and left chained to the rock, her youth wasting, her bloom arrested—the world merciless" (chapter 27).

In other words, in a Victorian broken marriage, the world would always pre-judge the woman and any attempt to find another partner would be bitterly scorned. She saw this all the more because it was happening to her beloved "Tony" and because she knew her to be sexually blameless, if very indiscreet, but still she saw it. Dacier rejects Diana utterly when he finds she has used a cabinet "secret" for reporter's copy and Meredith gives us an interesting diatribe on real women as opposed to the "marble block" of romance. "Diana was the flecked heroine of Reality; not always the same; not impeccable, not an ignorant-innocent, nor guileless; good under good leading; devoted to the death in a grave crisis" (chapter 35). Unfortunately, it is the last two phrases that grate on a modern ear: it seems that the hand of a good man is hinted at here in order to give a shove along the path of realistic character and strength of purpose! This leads me to a point that has often puzzled me and no doubt many others. If Meredith and other advanced writers could speak of reality in this way, are we to assume that all the other supremely virtuous maidens in Literature were being held up as moralistic examples solely. True, we read in Victorian autobiographies (and those of later date) that the "facts of life dawned slowly—often after marriage—upon such females, but "temptations" did not occur only to those in the know.

Thackeray points out that in the eighteenth-century young ladies may not have behaved more immorally or dishonestly, but they did not pretend not to know what went on—if one is to judge from the works of Richardson, Fielding, Dr. Johnson, and the letters of our ancestors. If similar books to *Clarisa* and *Roderick Random* were written in the nineteenth-century, he adds, "How the pure and outraged Nineteenth Century would blush, scream, run out of the room, call away the young ladies and order Mr. Mudie never to send one of that odious author's books again." To underline his satire, he adds a wondering comment that there are perhaps more Susannahs and fewer wicked elders in his times (*Virginians*, Part 1, chapter 41). Certainly Beatrix is a wicked old lady by now, but as she has danced through the pages of *Henry Esmond* and limped through the *Virginians*, we realise that Thackeray finds her a highly entertaining companion. Her selfishness rather than her immortality is more distasteful to him, it would seem.

Empty marriages, in which one partner can run riot in the sexual field while the other must stay at home and put on a brave face, are obviously not "approved" by Victorian moralists, but few writers are as outspoken about the woman's point of view as the gentle, unmarried Anne Bronte: no doubt because she had seen more than she cared to talk about to her sisters in her time as a governess. In *The Tenant of Wildfell Hall*, Helen Graham shows courage in saying "I will not be mocked by the empty husk of conjugal endearments when you have given the substance to another" (chapter 33). Later she is to say to Gilbert (and remember, she is very religious and this must be borne in mind even when written as late as 1892): "Don't you feel every interview makes you dearer to each other than the last?" And again "I have the power to make you go now but another time it might be different?" (chapter 45). Delicate phrasing, but the passage is loud and clear: especially as Gilbert has been arguing that in the sight of Heaven her husband has forfeited all claims on her. When we meet Mrs. Transome, George Eliot seems a little over-condemnatory of her youthful liaison with Mr. Jermyn, speaking of them "—indulging their passion and their vanity and determining for themselves how their lives should be made more delightful in spite of inalterable external conditions." Yet as the book progresses and we hear more of the lovelessness of Mrs. Transome's marriage (partly her own fault, in this case) at least we are given an insight that she does suffer, whereas Jermyn though married and with a family goes from strength to strength in business, with no sign of penitence for the past." The memory of all those years came back to her now with a protest against all the cruelty that had fallen on *her*! (*Felix Holt*, chapter 21 and chapter 50).

Some promiscuous husbands at that time could perhaps blame their conduct on wives who had no affection to give and with the number of "arranged" marriages in high society this would be fair comment. The sensible Hetta in *The Way We Live Now* (chapter 52) tells her mother that much as she knows Roger Carbury to possess "A soft heart and sweet nature-high honour," she "Did not know how she could give herself into the arms of a man she did not love." Lady Cadbury is something of a bully and Hetty knows that her brother's expenses are dooming her to a pretty grim spinsterhood (at that stage of the book), but at least she has the right sensitivities. Ethel Newcome, on the other hand, does not, although luckily Thackeray saves her from a loveless marriage. Certainly Ethel is more of a beauty, is more spoilt, is more tempted by wealth than Hetty, but the fact remains that both have equally worldly training by the relative closest to them. Presumably it is Hetty's love for Paul that saves her, but more likely that Victorian Morality did not enter into these marriage-bargains. They were literally a matter of "convenience." Thus Trollope was at liberty to show contempt in one way, Thackeray in another. The idea that one's parents knew best how to protect one from a foolish romance was a very thin smokescreen for the money-market aspect. Lucinda Rooke does not ogle men or appear to want their flirtations, yet her lack of prospects was still remarked by Society. "It must be presumed that Lucinda Rooke was in want of a husband and yet no girl took less pains to get one" *Eustace Diamonds*, chapter 36).

However, here Trollope has another method of bringing the thing to a stop. Groomed for heartlessness by her aunt, taking a lover would strike a false note for her, but when it came to her wedding day, she refused to leave her room and sent a message that she would kill her betrothed if he came near her again. Sensational stuff, but in fact Lucinda, though reckless in the hunting-field, has not shown any human emotions until this point. To revert to the man's side of such marriages, the Hartletops are appalled that their son should be marrying a mere Archdeacon's daughter. They must be aware their son is a roue, but they say among themselves that at least Griselda is "suitable" in that "She sees all she ought to see and nothing that she ought not" (*Framley Parsonage*, chapter 48).

Literary production in nineteenth-century England was a singularly complex development. There were many influences involved but moral, social, and economic issues and problems have inevitably influenced the intellectual and literary interests of male and female writers.

Utilitarianism was the dominant moral and political theory in England for a period of over a hundred years. The utilitarians were not without morals, but their conception of morality was egoistic, hedonistic, and class-orientated. They favoured the rich at the expense of the poor. They also lacked any positive conception of a social good. Jeremy

Bentham believed that the very notion of *summum bonum* is "absurd and mischievous." Self-interest or, what he calls, the principle of utility is the measure of right and wrong "in the field of morals." It is also the true standard of moral value and "the test and measure of all virtue."

Although Herbert Spencer's evolutionary utilitarianism differs in some respects from Bentham's egoistic utilitarianism, Spencer shares Bentham's view that pleasure is the test and measure of moral values. Actions are right only when they are "immediately pleasurable and wrong when painful." Spencer's evolutionary ethics, however, contains elements from both philosophical radicalism and Darwinism. Morality, he thinks, evolves like nature.

Bentham and Spencer were generally recognised as the most important exponents of utilitarianism in the nineteenth century. All utilitarians were aggressive, self-confident, egoistic and undemocratic. It is not surprising, therefore, that they were very unpopular among the lower classes as well as among many writers and moralists.

Thomas Green criticised Spencer's biological reductionism. Life, he thinks, cannot be the moral standard. The history of morality begins with the first appearance of reason, not with the first appearance of life. George Eliot also rejects the reduction of morality to biology and the utilitarian standard of right and wrong. In *Felix Holt*, she says that "it is not possible for any society in which there is a very large body of wise and virtuous men to be as vicious as our society is—to have a low standard of right and wrong, to have so much belief in falsehood, or to have so degrading, barbarous notion of what pleasure is."

In *Past and Present* Thomas Carlyle condemns the emptiness and hollowness of the Victorian age, which has alienated all social institutions. Cash-payment, he stresses, is not "the sole relation of human beings." He accuses the age of hypocrisy and lying. All talk about "competition, free-trade and laissez-faire is the shabbiest Gospel ever preached on earth." In the utilitarian social order, many are dying of inanition and the main sufferers are the poor classes.

Like Carlyle, Charles Dickens denounces both the soulless philosophy of Benthamite radicalism and the soulless philosophy of commercial fetishism. The image that haunts him in *Hard Times* is that of the worker who has nothing to do but mind a machine. Dickens satirises the political economists and utilitarian radicals for producing uncontrolled slums and proletariat and for discouraging poor people from relying on the system of poor relief.

Describing an industrial town in *Sybil*, Disraeli speaks of the lack of any public building—"no churches, chapels, town halls, institutes, theatre." The principal streets "in the heart of the town are narrow and dirty." The poor were helpless.

With the same passionate feeling for the poor, in *Mary Barton*, Elizabeth Gaskell deplores the suffering of the poor, which she ascribes to the indifferent cruelty of utilitarian economic laws. In the struggle to live humanly, the working classes are making enormous sacrifices, but their masters are ever-ready to exploit and alienate them.

In his criticism of James Mill's political economy—"the science of poverty"—Karl Marx deplores the fact that human morality, as expounded by Mill, has become "the object of commerce." He thinks that all utilitarian morality is a mockery of morality—"the immoral vileness of morality."

In addition to the utilitarian influence on moral and social orientation in nineteenth-century England, there was a strong influence of, what Max Werner calls, "the puritan ethic." According to him, the purital sects of the sixteenth and seventeenth centuries initiated the emergence of industrial capitalism and by stressing the connection between hard work, thrift, and religious salvation contributed to the growth of the "capitalist spirit."

Unlike traditional Christianity, which discouraged the accumulation of wealth, the puritan ethics saw riches as the reward for a life of diligence and thrift. According to the puritan ethics, human individuals exist for the sake of business and not the other way around. The qualities that less enlightened ages in the past denounced as moral vices and social evils became both moral and economic virtues. The attainment of material wealth was regarded as the supreme object of human endeavour and the final criterion of success. Being moral and becoming rich were seen as perfectly compatible moral terms.

Like George Eliot, Thomas Carlyle, and Elizabeth Gaskell, Charlotte Bronte condemns the miserable position of the poor in Victorian society. The dividing line between the rich and the poor is so great that the barrier between them might be impossible to transcend. In the Preface to *Jane Eyre*, C. Bronte rejects utilitarian "conventionalism," which wrongly assumed the role of Christian morality and kept women under the irrational domination of men. "Conventionality," she stresses, "is not morality. To attack the first is not to assail the last."

Victorian morality was certainly a negative phenomenon in society. It was egocentric, naturalistic, and deterministic. It was also abstract, fragmentary, and class-orientated. The lower orders of society as well as educated male and female writers categorically rejected Victorian morality because its advocates gave too much prominence to conventionalism and reduced the difference between virtue and vice, honesty and dishonesty, moral rectitude and wickedness to the difference between prudence and imprudence, or in short, to the principle of utility. Christian moralists and social reformers adhered to the view that morality should be based on reflective principles, not on blind customs and conventions.

# CHAPTER 7

# SPINSTERHOOD

On the face of it, in most Victorian novels, spinsterhood was to be avoided at all costs, but when you go closer, it is possible to find "cheerfulness breaking through"! In a word it seemed to be a state to be avoided but quite enviable if taken in the right spirit, accompanied by a reasonable income and above all a symbol of some sort of freedom. This freedom came late in life if a parent was either dependent on your services or dominating you even more than the most intractable husband!

Anne Bronte writes feelingly of Mary Millward: "A plain, quiet, sensible girl who had patiently nursed their mother through her last, long, tedious illness" (*Tenant of Wildfell Hall*, chapter 1) and later we read "Though in single life your joys may not be very many, at least your sorrows will not be more than you can bear" (chapter 41, ibid). A rather negative view, but at least a step away from marriage being a desperate and feverish search.

Charlotte Bronte put a different type of wording on a male character's lips because, unfortunately—even today—it is the masculine view of spinsterhood that is often the most contemptuous. "Old maids—the race whom all despise; they have fed themselves from youth upwards on maxims of resignation and endurance. Many of them get ossified with the dry diet. Self-control is so continually their thought, so perpetually their object that it at last absorbs the softer and more agreeable qualities" (*The Professor*, chapter 23).

Delightful! In other words, if no use to a man, they are no use to anyone? But, of course, it was not meant this way by the speaker, presumably—his surface meaning would have been something along the lines of a woman's greatest fulfillment being that of a wife and mother. Quite, why she should ossify to such an extent is sadly amusing when one considers the different tone taken regarding richer and politically or socially aware women, by other male characters in other fields.

Trollope in *The Kellys and the O'Kellys* comments on Selina finally remaining single. "—but her temper is not thereby soured nor her life embittered. She is active, energetic and as good as ever." This is not to say she is a saint; having been born "cold, harsh, harsh and dignified," she naturally remains so. This is not her reflection on single life but on the narrow class to which she belongs (chapter 39). Miss Dunstable is a woman by nature, "Kind, generous and open-hearted—she was clever also and could be sarcastic" (*Framley Parsonage*, chapter 17). However, we gradually see her goodness being eroded by scorn for those who admire her for her wealth alone. She has a few loved and loving friends, but marriage cannot appeal to her while she feels "used." She does in fact marry by the end of the book but at an age when she has already discredited the threadbare adjectives about spinsters—partly because she is very much a person in her own right but partly because the Victorian worship of money must have been most impressed by Miss Dunstable's skilful manipulation of business matters!

Miss Mitford gives a very contented picture of her own single state and even tells the story of two spinsters living together in which she gives a personal footnote "A union enduring—cemented by cheerfulness and good-humour" (*Village Tales*, Rosedale). These two ladies are contented despite low incomes, but in the case of Jane Gordon "Proposal after proposal had been rejected," because Jane's income is such that she can enjoy her independence. She does marry as it is a love-story, but Miss Mitford tells us that "I have seldom met with anyone who had a wider reach of thought, a purer taste, a warmer heart or a kinder temper" and yet her manner to suitors is "abundantly chilling" ("A Moonlight Adventure," from *Our Village*). It would be rather petty to suggest that Jane's vast fortune alone keeps her contended because until she meets the young hero, she is contented with pursuits of the mind that most young men do not even suspect women capable of. When Miss Mitford is passing through the village after a visit away from home, she sees signs of a recent village wedding, but on return to her own cottage, she says "The dear, dear home! No weddings here! No changes! Except that white kitten has superceded his lamented grandfather, our beautiful Persian cat, I can not find one change to speak of (Another Glance: *Our Village*). There is no sour grapes here; one has to digest the flavour of the whole book to find the utter contentment—not a Miss Matty-like resignation"—because her writings, though limited, obviously fulfill her life, together with deep love of human observation.

She slyly counteracts any would-be jokes on "old maids" by telling us the story of Mrs. Sally being able to pick up a flail and demonstrate the old ways of threshing, with great muscular energy, at sixty-five! The "Mrs." is a courteous title and although tending to be a prude when young, she now takes up habitation with a farmer Robinson on a severely platonic basis, but "To be sure, upon the verge of seventy an old maid may be permitted to dispense with the more rigid punctilio of her class" ("*The Copse*," from *Our Village*). The early farming ways of this good lady obviously lead not only to a full life when young and contented memories when old—marriage is not of great consequence to her.

In *Shirley*, we see two approaches—Caroline Helstone intends to face up to singleness in a positive manner because she foresees that Robert may marry the rich heiress. Shirley <u>enjoys</u> a single life because she is in command of a thriving business, has many artistic interests and because, at that point of the book, she is heart-whole. To return to Caroline—thinking over the common role of spinsters, she muses: "Other people solve it for them by saying 'Your place is to do good to others, to be helpful where help is wanted.' —Is this enough? Is it to live? Is there not a terrible hollowness, mockery, want, craving, in that existence, which is given away to others, for want of something of your own to bestow it on? This, she decides, is not good enough as "Every human being has his share of rights. I suspect it would conduce to the happiness and welfare of all, if each knew his allotment, and held to it as tenaciously as the martyr to his creed" (chapter 10). But when she is left alone after accustoming herself to Shirley's new friendship (as Shirley has gone north to visit relatives), she puts her philosophy into more practical shape in her thoughts. "I believe single women should have more to do—better chances of interesting and profitable occupation than they possess now—the brothers of these girls are every one in business or in professions; they have something to do; their sisters have no earthly employment, but household work and sewing" (chapter 22). Shirley, on the other hand, scorns the idea of marriage as an aim in life, rather than bothering too much about possible empty future. Perhaps like the Emma of an earlier writer, she realises it is only the Miss Bates's of this life who need dread the future, not the rich heiresses. "If I find out that they" (men) "are necessarily fickle, soon petrifying, unsympathising—I would never marry I would not like to find that what I loved did not love me"—and, more to the point, she is to add in summing up "Now, when I feel my company superfluous, I can comfortably fold my independence round me like a mantle, and drop my pride like a veil and withdraw to solitude" (chapter 12).

Attitudes to single women are often based on rather weird to us premises. Frank Greystock shows a certain shallowness in remarking "How odd it is to think of two women living alone in a great house like that," adding, "the truth is that women don't do well alone. There is always a savour of misfortune — or at least of melancholy — about a household that has no man to look after it. With us, generally old maids don't keep houses and widows marry again" (*Eustace Diamonds*, chapter 25). He is puzzled, basically by the emptiness of women's lives, but mistakenly attributes it to lack of men rather than the lack of occupation. Trollope himself sarcastically remarks in *The Way We Live Now* that "Nothing is so efficacious in preventing men from marrying as the tone in which married women speak of the struggles of their unmarried friends in that direction" (chapter 32). This particular bitchiness of course can be found today among some of our contemporaries who can be amusing, after their fashion, on the same score! Being "on the shelf" may, on the other hand, be used in a half-joking context today (for instance men will be heard to say it lightly of themselves), but evidently it was a very serious matter to some young Victorian women. Georgiana Longstaffe is not a very pleasant person, but there is a certain pathos in the fact that she dreads going to London to stay with rich but somewhat "shady" people. Yet as her father cannot afford to take the girls to Town, she feels she must go. "It is the only chance left. If I were to remain down here everybody would say I was on the shelf" (*The Way We Live Now*, chapter 21). Unpleasant Georgiana may be, but she is an intelligent girl and in a different century would have put her gifts to good uses, but Trollope says pitying, "It is difficult for a young lady to break off with her family. A young woman may go anywhere — may demand an allowance and has almost a right to live alone — but the daughter of a house is compelled to adhere to her father till she shall get a husband" (Ibid, chapter 78). These thoughts are aroused by Georgiana's bitter remark that she had done with them all, when her father forcibly breaks off her engagement to a City Jew much older than herself. Georgiana has been schooled for so long that marriage was a condition of things that had to be brought about by her own efforts that "It was beyond the scope of her mind to contemplate the chances of a life in which marriage may be well if it came, but in which unmarried tranquillity might also be well" (*The Way We Live Now*, chapter 95). An admirable doctrine, the latter, but unfortunately not one sufficiently glowingly painted by many writers! It is almost as if a character has to be at rock-bottom before her creator (particularly if male, but not always) hastily recalls it. The sad and savage Lucinda Ronaoake almost gives us a preview of the debâcle of her wedding-day when she says to her aunt (who is expatiating on a girl in a play who cannot make up her mind regarding which man to marry) "But may one not have an idea of no man at all?" (Trollope: *Eustace Diamonds*, chapter 52).

Spinsterhood, we see, is regarded quite benignly if one is already over thirty, has a comfortable income or a "use" in life, but a feverish avoidance of the state seems to be the order of the day between sixteen and thirty! On the other hand, an equally feverish search for a husband is evidently bad taste. So, unless the heroine is very beautiful or very rich, or both, a bit of an impasse seems to be reached.

# CHAPTER 8

# STRENGTH OF CHARACTER

Despite the limitations we have seen imposed in previous chapters by the general male attitude, the exigencies of marriage, the mockery of spinsterhood, and the stringencies of morality, many authors are aware of something ticking away in the dark: women's frequent strength of purpose and will that was bound to result in their emancipation, one day. That this determination was not turned at this point to Votes for Women and related subjects is irrelevant. The fact remains that the charming but cringing puppy dog image of women is beginning to get on the nerves of most writers.

George Eliot is naturally a promoter of women of spirit but of course realises they do not always get the opportunity to display it. A certain winsome wilfulness has attracted but annoyed both Felix Holt and the reader when they first know Esther, but when she stands up in court, spontaneously to defend Felix, "Some of the ardour which has flashed out and illuminated all History was burning today in Esther Lyon." Coy awareness of her sex is forgotten; that men are looking at her no longer crosses her mind (*Felix Holt*, chapter 46). This may be seen as a dramatic example, which Esther did not necessarily sustain, but other female characters are "real" throughout a novel by nature of their very strength. Married women, of course, are often given a little leeway by their creators — Mrs. Carey in Disraeli's *Sybil* is very outspoken and what is more interesting, she is more realistic than many other female characters therein: interesting in that the author seems to say "This is what we meet; not what mealy-mouthed readers would like us to meet in everyday life." When Mrs. Carey tells the youth who contemptuously dismisses his mother as not dying, but drunk "And if she is only drunk, what makes her drink, but toil? Working from midnight five o'clock in the morning to seven o'clock at night, and for the like of such as you" (chapter 3). "Dandy Mick," as the factory girls call him, cheeks her back, but throughout the chapter, one sees that a woman who has to do business at a huckster's stall and fight her way through life can only gain admiration. A moment of pathos is struck when the girls are telling her of the schools set up by Trafford's Mills. Mrs. Carey remarks "Learning is better than house or lands, though I'm no scholar myself." Another interesting character of similar "low birth" but with plenty of obviously admired guts—admired, certainly, by the author was Miss Barbara Jennings. Having bought, with her friend, Laura, a cottage in the country after years of "servitude" to an aunt in London, she expects it to consist of all the amenities one associates with romantic spots. No live-stock being supplied, she bought them and housed them in unusual spots such as the little brewery and the orangery! The gardener (infuriated by the animals cropping on the lawn) summoned the lawyer armed with lease. Barbara "Cried, scolded, reasoned and implored." When the lawyer forced his point, "She would have marched off at the same time" (i.e., back to London) if a kindly farmer's wife had not offered to let the creatures Barbara had grown fond of "board" with her! ("Rosedale," from *Our Village*). Although described earlier as "vulgar" by Miss Mitford, she has obviously been left a bit of money by her demanding aunt, but, though this may have brought out her latent strength of character, it must always have been there. The sense of duty to relatives dinned into maiden ears by Victorian moralists, often only liberated the spirited ones in later life.

Returning to higher Society, one is frequently irritated by the misuse Ethel Newcome puts her strong will to petulance, hauteur, mistaken pride, and so on. The general idea seems to be that if her grandmother desires a rich, well-connected marriage for her, so be it, but she will not accept the first one that comes. However, when a situation calls for strong character in doing something right, even if the niceties of the situation override Society's rules, Ethel does not hesitate to act. She goes to see the colonel despite the relatives' general haughty attitude towards him, when he is returning to India." As for Ethel, she was not going to be put off by this sort of parting: and the next morning a cab dashed up to Fitzroy Square and a veiled lady came out" (Thackeray: *The Newcomes*, chapter 26). Of course, the veiled aspect seems absurd to us, especially when the gentleman concerned is elderly. But a moment's thought tells us that the spirit underlying this action is still of the "stand up and be counted" nature. Trollope obviously sees that women of character, no matter how spoilt by twisted upbringing, act as men when the crux comes. The trouble is that frequently, scenting power, women once married become petty tyrants, if one is to believe some writers. Or do women of character think 'Rule or be ruled'? Thackeray speaks, half-laughingly, that "If women care to exert their wills they could conquer men in the early days of marriage." He goes on to cite a certain Parson Blake who was once a Redcoat and was "The fire-eater of the forty-third" but now he sees his match "In his own home and one glance from his wife" (prevents) "him daring to face a glass of old port wine" (*Virginians*, part 2, chapter 23). Shrews, of course, are not what Women's Equality is about, but I am seeking more for indications that women did not sit about and "vapourise" as readers might imagine from lighter fiction or from their own general impressions of such heroines as Dora Copperfield or Amelia Sedley. In the 1980s, there may not be a career woman in every nagging wife "fighting to get out" (nagging may indeed be her fort, even if she was a career woman!) but there is no reason to suppose that things may not have been very different in the last century.

Emergencies were shown to bring out strong traits in certain women. When Ruth is very ill, Miss Benson takes over the sick-room with great determination. Now this is not surprising in itself: the little woman, soothing fevered brows, is one we are all familiar with in Victorian fiction, but something else emerges. "Miss Benson had the power, which some people have, of carrying her wishes through to their fulfillment; her will was strong, her sense was excellent, and people yielded to her—they did not know why" (Gaskell: *Ruth*, chapter 11). Reading on, one gains the impression that if Miss Benson saw something needed doing in other fields besides nursing, matters would have been the same. "Unwomanly pursuits" do not arise, as no training would have been available, anyway! Leonora Franklin in "Life's Little Ironies: For Conscience Sake" sees no point in marrying her old lover for respectability's sake when she has a thriving music teacher position together with a piano-hiring business. "My position in this town is a respected one; I have built up out of my own hard labours, and, in short, I don't wish to alter it." The spirited girl sees no point in marriage for its own sake, just because Millbourne has a pang about having seduced her twenty years previously! These stories were written by Hardy between 1888 and 1893, so obviously things are moving on a bit, but not in a manner welcomed by all authors necessarily.

Mary Garth inherits from her mother a great independence of nature. We read that Mrs. Garth learned in her youth to suppress a tendency to sarcasm not as a matter of submission but of self-discipline

(*Middlemarch*, chapter 24) and Mary has earlier observed, "I do like to be spoken to as if I had commonsense. I really feel as if I could understand a little more than I ever hear from young gentlemen who have been to College" (Ibid, chapter 14). Admittedly she laughs a little at poor Fred after saying this, but fond as she secretly is of him, she obviously still feels very much a human being in her own right. In the famous scene where Mary waits by her uncle's sick-bed, we read that she is a girl who likes to be alone with her thoughts. Her philosophy of life is not one arising from bitterness, as might at first appear, but of great realism. "She had already come to take life very much as a comedy in which she had a generous resolve not to act the mean or treacherous part." Mary might have become cynical if she had not had parents whom she had honoured and—had learned not to make unreasonable claims (i.e., of life) (chapter 33).

Being thrown on the mercies of life was also a justification for a little womanly force of character. Perhaps wearied by the "sweetness" of Rosa Budd (although she is to show more individuality when up against it), Dickens gives us Helena. She is supposedly somewhat wild, as is her brother, because of the cruel upbringing of their father in India. She is quick to derive great intellectual benefit from Mr. Crisparkle. This is passed *indirectly* through her brother's coaching from the latter. Mr. Crisparkle notices that whatever he teaches, the boy is absorbed immediately to the girl. Tigress-like allusions are sometimes made to poor Helena, but she is quick to tame that nature when she perceives the innate goodness and honesty beneath the childish shallowness of Rosa (*Edwin Drood*, chapters 9 & 10). Therefore, strength of personality is allowable if one has circumstances that dictate it. When it militates against your chances of marriage, however, that is another thing! It does not seem odd to Mrs. Carbunkle—a sophisticated woman—to speak of her niece as requiring "breaking in" by marriage. "At the pension in Paris, they couldn't break her in at all." No wonder such places were called "Finishing schools" and no wonder the haughty Lucinda Ronaoake balked on her actual wedding-day! Having a mind of one's own all too often seemed to culminate in ruthlessness or eventual unhappiness. To instance the first: Lydia Esmond, the American heiress, is witty and outspoken, sees through falsity and generally "does her own thing." Ha, ha, one might think a real young woman at last. Then she spoils it all—for George Warrington first of all—by speaking of the old thus "When they come to that, people oughtn't to live" (*Virginians*, Part 2, chapter 73).

To illustrate the other point, Ethelberta shows great self-control for one so naturally emotional in relating stirring tales to an audience, to add to her fame as a poet. Hardy remarks rather tartly: "A talent for demureness under difficulties without the cold-bloodnessness which renders such a bearing natural and easy—is a constitutional arrangement much to be desired by people in general; yet, had Ethelberta been framed with less of a gift in her her life might have been more comfortable as an experience and brighter as an example" (*The Hand of Ethelberta*, chapter 16). Hardy, enlightened as he was for his times, does not seem to consider the fact that such iron nerves would hardly be necessary in the possession or the pretence if Society had been less amazed at new ways of young women earning their livings. As I have remarked before, married women could get away with more and therefore forcible widows sometimes, particularly if wealthy, are very distinctive people. Rachel Esmond is forceful throughout *The Virginians* and, admittedly, this takes the unpleasant form of unforgiving pride towards her elder son, but when it comes to patriotism, she does not even pause to consider whether she be male or female. Having persuaded a young aide-de-camp to strike "Britons Strike Home!" during the day of fasting and prayer after the Boston Ball, she leans out of the window when the people throw stones shouting the same words "in chorus" (chapter 86).

Thackeray, of course, throughout this novel is referring back to a previous century, but his tone is such that he obviously expects a Victorian reader to feel complete empathy. Eleanor Bold one would assume to live in another world from Mrs. Esmond as she is seen as clinging like ivy to the oak of John Bold, but when it comes to matters she feels in the right about, she is quite another person. Archdeacon Grantley may intimidate others, but Eleanor is very strong in her views about him. "He is so uncharitable, so unkind, so suspicious of every one that does not worship himself; and then he is so monstrously arrogant to other people who have a right to their opinions as well as he to his own" (Trollope: *Barchester Towers*, Vol. 2, chapter 28).

Easy to say all this to her gentle father, someone might remark, but she is to be equally frank with her brother-in-law both when he rebukes her for being kind to Slope and even more so when he admonishes her for receiving a letter from him—all this because she feels herself to be in the right. Independent financial resources no doubt made it easy for her, as she can leave Grantley's house if provoked, but one gains the impression that once the depths of her character were stirred, she would not have laid low even if dependent on him. When Slope does finally propose and puts his arm round her, she slaps him without hesitation. Trollope jokingly remarks that this may be considered "hoydenish" behaviour by his readers but that "She was too keen in the feeling of independence" (Ibid, chapter 56).

In *The Egoist*, Clara Middleton struggles for another type of independence—a mental one. She pictures Willoughby being whipped as a boy (the mere thought a sacrilege to his aunts) and realises that even to mock such a man in her thoughts was denied her. "She asked for some little, only some little free play of mind in a house that seemed to wear, as it were, a cap of iron" (Meredith: *The Egoist*, chapter 9). The "cap of iron" metaphor is repeated in the same paragraph and we see that Willoughby is not so much a bully as so inordinately spoilt that even his male cousin desists from contradicting him. Meredith has remarked in a previous paragraph that spirited young women hesitate before throwing in their lot with a person that male society and the more rigid matrons think eminently respectable, even if obsessively sensitive to criticism. When Clara is later thinking how horrified Society would be if she went back on her engagement, she luckily has the strength of character to think that nothing worse could be done by any woman than to sign themselves over by oath and ceremony, because of an ignorant promise, to a man they have been mistaken in" (Ibid, chapter 10).

Downright unpleasant women or outright villainesses are allowed all the strength of character anyone could wish for and how interesting this often makes them! Madame Beck has such strength of character that she "Ought to have ruled nations; she should have been the leader of a legislative assembly" (*Villette*, chapter 8). Yet, basically one doesn't feel that Charlotte Bronte would consider a bad thing for a woman to hold these positions; it is more that her personal memories of Madame Heger are so bitter. The Miss Proudies may be infinitely dislikeable but it is evidently not considered a surprise to the Victorian reader that they have "wills of their own which become stronger every day" (*Framley Parsonage* chapter 6). Mrs. Harold Smith has not married for love and at home," She managed to keep the upper hand—in a manner that made her rule bearable" (Ibid, chapter 24).

Politically and in the generally shady world her husband inhabits, she more than holds her own, so it is a pity that this is to be seen as a "bad thing" since many women may have longed to express equal gifts in an honorable manner. It would take too long to analyse such "villainesses" as Becky Sharp or Lizzie Eustace in detail, but certainly they were capable of anything to gain their own ends. Yet in another world, how their quick-wittedness, their sense of humour, their forthrightness (when free to express it), their manipulative powers would have led them on and on in a business or professional field. Lizzie is called lazy on several occasions by her creator. Yet this seems merely to indicate she could not be bothered to pursue her latest fad: be it poetry or French to great lengths—but immense vitality was put into her financial wranglings! Beatrix Castlewood, of course, had a strong character in a sense but would probably be the polished and witty courtizan-type in any generation. Her handling of money affairs showed an admirable grasp, but her interest in men or admiration of herself amounted to much more in life. Becky and Lizzie were not basically interested in men, except as a means to an end and being admired was not as important as keeping one's head above water and generally making sure, each in her different way, of a cosy future!

To sum up: strong character was not over-encouraged in the heroines of Victorian Literature unless it was called for in rearing a family single-handed or in manipulating a vast fortune. Bravery, forthright speech, and a limited amount of individuality was welcomed as a refreshing change from wishy-washiness. That strong characters awaited, ready to spring, in real life was more than hinted at. In a way one is reminded of Lucy Morris pointing out to her sister-in-law that one cannot await a proposal before finding out if you love someone although Lady Lufton seems to think when class is involved one should! (*Framley Parsonage*, chapter 31). In the same way, some authors seem to feel that strength of character is a commodity that a nice girl should keep handy and very restrained for suitable emergencies.

# CHAPTER 9

# THE POLITICAL EMERGENCE OF WOMEN

Obviously before a section of the community can "emerge" politically, its members have to be politically *aware*. It would be pointless for others to work for them if they were not interested. Nevertheless, as with universal manhood suffrage, the two can go hand in hand but not always in step! Different decades throw up different attitudes in literature and it is of that we are speaking.

Lady Glencora is half-joking, but she is genuinely goaded when she says, "Well, I suppose I may have my political sympathies as well as another—I shall have to go for women's rights" (*The Prime Minister* chapter 32). She mentions in passing that it is her husband's autocratic attitude that causes this mood, but one feels she still speaks for her sex. Lady Marney in *Sybil* is a strange mixture: she manipulates things, feeling she has the pulse of matters at her fingertips—yet half-despises the "corruptions" she senses in the House. In chapter 4, she speaks openly of the sort of practices that go on, admitting the middle classes want Reform, that probably the Liberals had preached the same thing in Walpole's time. She implies it is a pity reform is not on its way, but since it isn't, "I shall go down and canvass—we must do what we can" (In chapter 5). Disraeli calls her "A distinguished states-woman, as they called Lady Carlisle in Charles I's time"). Sybil herself has "the quick intelligence and ardent imagination" to follow the cause of "the oppression of her Church and the degradation of her people," but those same powers of mind lead her to find out that "Great thoughts have little to do with the business of the World" (*Sybil*, Book 5, chapter 1). Sybil is a rather wooden, over-idealised character, but she does her best by reading Westminster journals to keep up with debates and understand how things tick. The working girls Julia and Caroline have less educational background but are more in touch with reality when they say they have rights to discuss a Working Man's Charter and, in fact, Caroline states that she would never marry a man who did not "—agree to the five points." Harriet, another friend, says "I would be ashamed to marry any man who has not the suffrage." This, a modern reader may feel, is hardly a blow for women's rights, but Harriet is later to state, "As for that, why are we not to interfere with politics just as much as the swell ladies in London?" When the Widow Carey demurs, although a spirited lady in her own way, Julia retorts, "There was no March of Mind then" (i.e., in the widow's youth) "But we know the time of day now as well as any of them." The phrase "March of Mind" was a cant one printed in a Worker's manual published by Lord Russell and others. But the fact remains that for all her poor education, Julia's sharp mind knew what she was talking about. (*Sybil* Book 6, chapter 8). Shirley, as one might expect, has very forthright views on politics, as in everything else. She speaks hotly on her tenant's behalf when Moore engages soldiers to quell a riot. Mr. Yorke, smiling, suggests she should be more cool, and she indignantly replies, "Cool. Must I listen to downright nonsense—to dangerous nonsense?" After decrying a lot of middle-class views as "cant," she continues: "All ridiculous crying up of one class against another, whether the same be aristocratic or democratic—all exacting of injustice to individuals, whether monarch or mendicant—is sickening to me." Although very detached to Mr. Yorke, she goes on to tell him he only imagines himself a philanthropist but that Mr. Hall the parson is "a better friend both of man and freedom, than Hiram Yorke, the Reformer of Briarfield."

More interestingly still, after a pause, she exposes at length her views that most men, were they ever to be Prime Minister, would abandon their ideals almost immediately. She brings it all to a conclusion by suggesting as to whether men exist sufficiently merciful and reasonable to be trusted with reform. She is so vehement one is left with the question in the air as to whether she would think women could do it better.

Writing in 1849 and without Disraeli's great political knowledge, Charlotte Bronte may not feel that a burning issue—but knowing Shirley's own views on women's abilities to do most things better than men, she might have pursued the subject had not Mr. Yorke sarcastically suggested that a wedding date might be imminent between herself and Robert Moore. (*Shirley*, chapter 21). This was a little uncalled for, as she had just pointed out that Moore was only minimally more just and kind than other employers, but Yorke, hurt by what he feels are unjust accusations against his master-servant attitude, wants to suggest that a young lady can only be interested in a young man if she is interested in him!

I have already mentioned under "Intellectual Potential" that Meredith felt (in *Rhoda Fleming*) that there was "A democratic virus" at work in most women that enabled them to see that the rights of individual manhood were to be recognised in defiance of station and all the other impositions of Society. Men, therefore, had to do the forging ahead first, in his mind before women could get started. Poor Mrs. Wilson in *Mary Barton* wonders whether Prince Albert would like it if his wife had to work the hours that factory women worked (chapter 10). One senses the burning desire to put things as they really were to the powers that be—but what a terrible pathos in the thought that with a woman on the throne and a strong-willed one, it is to the husband of that Queen Mrs. Wilson would appeal! Mary does point out that surely it was the Queen who made the laws. Mrs. Wilson agrees but says she is still bound to obey Prince Albert. "So, why can't he make a law against poor folk's wives working in factories?"

In *Coningsby*, Lord Eskdale points out that they had made a mistake about the ladies and continues: "Male firmness is often obstinacy; women have something much better worth all the qualities; they have tact." As women had to vote, he is obviously referring to the necessity to listen to women, if they are politically aware. Lady Everingham shows the quality of mind required. "An Opposition in an Age of Revolution must be founded on principles. It cannot depend on mere personal qualities and party address taking advantage of circumstances. You have not enunciated a principle for the last eight years and when you seemed on the point of acceding to power it was not on a great question of national interest but a technical dispute respecting the condition of some run-down sugar colony" (speaking to Lord Fitzbooby. Disraeli: *Coningsby*, Book 8, chapter 1).

# CHAPTER 10

# PHILANTHROPY

There is no need to remind those whose toes curl up at the word or thought of "do-gooding" that there was no Lloyd George Health Benefits, no National Healthy even with all its faults, in the days we are contemplating. In considering the Benevolence that came from women, one naturally looks at those with as little condescension as possible—leaving the Mrs. Pardiggles and Mrs. Jellybys to remain in the realms of farce where they rightly belong.

George Eliot's Dorothea naturally springs to mind as her natural fervour, tenderheartedness, and command over her own funds would find outlet in public generosity. She sets up a school in the village and visits it regularly—no patronising manner here (*Middlemarch*, chapter 1). When she talks to James Chettam about the condition of Mr. Brooke's Labourers' cottages, she has a tone of sincerity, which the author does not grant to hypocrites. "We deserve to be whipped out of our beautiful houses with a scourge of small cords—all of us who let our tenants live in such sties as we see around us. Life in cottages might be happier than ours if they were real houses fit for human beings" (chapter 3). The last sentence might seem a little unrealistic if we did not know that Dorothea is the sort of girl who would be happy in a comfortable cottage. As we follow her through the book, we find that she cannot be happy when she sees money wasted, as she feels, on endless paintings, when so much poverty exists. "I should like to make life beautiful—I mean everybody's life. And then all this immense expense of Art that seems to lie outside life and makes it no better for the World, pains one." Obviously, it cannot be expected to pain Will, to whom she is speaking. He hopes to make his living from Art and suggests that she would only curb some people's pleasure, bringing no great advantage to her own happiness (chapter 22). Remembering that Dorothea is only bored by her many visits to Galleries and Museums in

Rome, a reader may justifiably feel that she should "put her money where her mouth is," i.e., spare some of her fortune where it does hurt her. Now, in the early days of marriage to Casaubon, she is more than anxious to please him, so we can assume that it is painful to her to argue over fairness to his cousin. "My own money brings me nothing but an uneasy conscience." She cries out when wondering if her husband will ever fully realise that the Ladislaw family have been wrongly treated in the past by his own (chapter 37). That her husband might already have the stirrings of jealousy against Will certainly doesn't cross her mind, since one also reads that her own property possession has irked for a long time. When she visits her uncle to discuss his prospecting for Parliament, she is eager to show him the passionate need for an enlightened member. She suggests forthrightly that he should get started by employing Garth to improve the cottages, mentioned earlier. "She chanted as a credo 'You mean to enter Parliament as a member who cares for the improvement of the people and one of the first things to be made better is the state of the land and the labourers.' " She then lists individual families with exact details of their poverty and sufferings showing that this is not just fine talk—she has been there and found out. (chapter 39). Later, when the hospital plans are under discussion, she immediately wishes to help. Speaking to Lydgate, she remarks, "I have some money I don't know what to do with—it is often an uncomfortable thought to me. I am sure I can spare two hundred a year for a grand purpose like this. How happy you must be (i.e., as a doctor) to know things you feel sure will do great good! I wish I could awake each morning with that knowledge" (chapter 44).

When she is a widow and Mrs. Cadwallader irritates her by arch references to remarriage, she says indignantly to Celia, "I shall never marry again. I should like to take a great deal of land and drain it, and make a little colony where everyone should work and where all the work should be done well and I should know everyone of these people and be their friends. I am going to have great consultations with Mr. Garth—." Mr. Garth tells his wife of these schemes and finds them very practical, remarking that she had a great head for business.

George Eliot remarks ironically that by "business" Caleb did not mean finances but the skilful application of labour—but then why not? He was the struggling man of skill and she had the money, so no doubt lawyers could settle in the seeming impracticality of both speakers (chapters 45 & 46). In the last chapter, we hear that Dorothea, married to Will, "Has a life filled with beneficent activity." She has given up her fortune, but that still we can surmise leaves her enough to do the greatest good where the greatest need is.

I turn now to women with less to give, but whose impulses and actions are just as warm. Sybil visits the sick woman who without any malice says, "Your father deserves his good fortune with such a daughter" to which Sybil replies, "My father's fortunes are not much better than his neighbours but his wants are few; and who should sympathise with the poor but the poor? Alas! None else can." Sybil explains also that the actual food comes from the Convent where she is living, but what her father can do for the sick Mrs. Warner he will do.

In the same way, the "hopeless" look of the workmen is noticed and deeply cared about by Margaret. "In the South we have our poor but there is not that terrible expression of a sullen sense of injustice which I see here" (*North and South*, chapter 10). She cannot bear to hear Mr. Thornton boasting of wonderful progress and inventions in the North if it is to bring such pain. As a single girl, now in the area, she can hardly insult these workmen by handing them out indiscriminate charity and pitying words, but her concern is always with them and their families. In another Mrs. Gaskell's novel, *Sylvia* is unaware that she is ministering to her maimed lost husband, but it is because she remembers her mother's "Gentle superstition which had ever prevented her from sending the empty away for fear that she herself should come to need bread" (*Sylvia's Lovers*, chapter 44). Little Dorrit gave to whomever she could, including poor Maggie, but her scrimping of course had to be for her useless father as he appeared, to her, to be in need because of his wretched "better days" that he never ceased to repent.

Nevertheless, it obviously had to be those who had a surplus who could give to their neighbour the most. Shirley, when told by Caroline that she already gives more than generously even by the standards of the critical Mr. Helstone, retorts violently, "Not enough; I must give more, or, I tell you, my brother's blood will some day be crying to Heaven against me" (Charlotte Bronte: *Shirley*, chapter 14).

Being the honest girl she is, she openly admits that if her property is attacked, she will defend it fiercely. But "I cannot forget that these embittered feelings of the poor against the rich have been generated in suffering. — let me out of my abundance, give abundantly" (*Shirley*, chapter 14).

A very different type of woman: Rachel Warrington is naturally generous. "If ever a slave was ill she would go to his quarters in any weather and doctor him with great resolution" (*Virginians*, Part 1, chapter 4). Pointless to comment here on the fiendishness of having slaves at all, if one recalls that even George Washington did not noticeably improve the conditions of his household slaves, as any visitor to Mount Vernon can see for himself.

Ethel Newcome is another surprising person. With all her wilfulness and seeming indifference to the human race, she has a tender attitude to life's unfortunates. She not only visits Clive's old nurse (whom Lady Kew and Barnes sneer at), but she feels that Clive himself "Could not be very bad who was so kind and thoughtful for the poor" (*Newcomes*, Part 1, chapter 21). Moreover Ethel cannot bear her grandmother's treatment of her invalid Aunt Julia. She is always kind to her herself and once flashes out at her grandmother, "Keep them (*Bad Names*) for my Aunt Julia; she is sick and weak and can't defend herself" (Part I, chapter 34). Much of her personal fortune went towards the alleviation of the sufferings of the poor. "She gave much time and thought to them; visited from house to house without ostentation' (Book 2, chapter 62).

She is a freer agent by this time; but it is not a question of being a reformed character—this is obviously what is underneath the nature her grandmother tried to distort. Interestingly enough in another novel (*Pendennis*), Thackeray seeks to argue that men can't go through with too much empathy. "The mere changes and recurrence of grief and mourning would be intolerable." But the nature of good women—"putting such, no doubt, on far higher pedestal than modern tastes require—is to do kind offices and devise untiring charities" (chapter 74).

In *Life's Little Ironies: A Tragedy of Two Ambitions*, Mrs. Felmer, the mother of the Squire, "Did her almsgiving in person" and "Walked about the village even on very wet days visiting the parishioners." Easy to feel this is condescending, but Hardy makes it clear that she feels no such emotion and would think herself a very poor human being if she didn't do this.

The nineteenth century was a period of slow but increasing political and social reform in England. There was a general awakening of conscience, a realisation that the misery of the lower classes generated by unrestricted competition should be stopped. In *A New View of Society* in 1813, Robert Owen wrote that men and women should aim at happiness rather than wealth. He denounced egoistic individualism and advocated practical benevolence and philanthropy. He hoped to change the whole basis of social life and insisted that people should work unselfishly for the common good.

The Chartist movement, which drew the bulk of its support from dissatisfied workers, was hopelessly divided in its social programme. Owen and many trade unionists distrusted political and social aims of Chartism and refused to support it. Later in the century, however, the ideals of the Chartists inspired much of the progress relating to the democratisation of social structures. Both the Democratic Federation founded in 1881 and the Fabian Society founded in 1883 advocated the principle of benevolence in opposition to Bentham's egoistic principle of utility.

Bentham believed that "no human act can ever be disinterested." To him, philanthropy is essentially egoism in disguise. The only obligation man has, he says, is "the duty to himself." This attitude is shared by Spencer who holds that suffering is good and that "the creature not strong enough must die." In his puritan mood, he makes sarcastic remarks about philanthropy. Spencer speaks of "permanent supremacy of egoism over altruism." There is no room in Bentham's and Spencer's utilitarianism for philanthropy or charity. It is this attitude that has inspired the formulation of the Poor Laws and has led to the erroneous belief that all poverty is the fault of the poor.

Commenting on Bentham's conception of philanthropy, J. S. Mill says that "general philanthropy, considered as a motive influencing mankind in general, Bentham estimated at its true value when divorced from the feeling of duty—as the very weakest and most unsteady of all feelings." In Bentham's utilitarian philosophy, fellow feeling is subordinated to self-interest. Self-sacrifice, he says, is "neither possible nor desirable."

According to St. Thomas Aquinas, charity or benevolence or philanthropy is a virtue that "consists in loving rather than in being loved." By contrast, Luther had little regard for philanthropy. He denounced the demands of beggars as blackmail. Citing with approval the words of St. Paul, "If a man will not work, neither shall he eat," Calvin also condemned indiscriminate almsgiving as strongly as any utilitarian.

In the nineteenth century, the Nonconformist religious sects formed with liberal radicalism a "working alliance" in which the mingling of spiritual and secular elements lent itself to parody. The sects provided an element of Christian charity that was lacking in the egoistic utilitarian ethics and in classical economics. Many male and female writers denounced this alliance in strongest terms. Matthew Arnold advocated "Christian charity" in its pure form and rejected the utilitarian attempt to modify its true practical value.

In *Past and Present*, Thomas Carlyle attacks the hypocrisy of Victorian society, stressing that the rich lack altogether any sympathy for the suffering of the poor and weak. He mentions "a forlorn Irish widow who applied to her fellow creatures for help. . . . Behold I am sinking, bare of help: your must help me! I am your sister, bone of your bone; one God made us: you must help me! The rich answered: No, impossible, you are no sister of ours." For Carlyle and Arnold, sympathy or philanthropy is the direct and substantive law of the moral life.

A similar conception of sympathy or philanthropy permeates Dickens's writings. In *Hard Times*, which he dedicated to Carlyle, Dickens attacks the social system, which is drawn up on strict egoistic utilitarian principles. He has no patience with "the coldly and bitingly emphatic train master" who extolled Political Economy, insisting that sympathy or philanthropy is totally irrelevant to economic problems. As the satirist and critic of political economy and utilitarianism, Dickens advocates generosity and fellow-feeling for suffering in all forms, whether caused by poverty, cruelty, sickness or injustice.

On the whole, female writers are more philanthropic and more genuinely sympathetic towards the suffering of the poor and to those in need. Many philosophers, psychologists, and social anthropologists, including Charles Darwin, confirm this view. One of the chief qualities of Elizabeth Gaskell's writings is her clear realism and objective analysis of the existing class-divided society. When she describes Margaret's singing of "The Oldham Weaver" in *Mary Barton*, she is describing her own sympathetic feeling towards the poor. Like the poor cotton weaver, Gaskell had both witnessed the destitution and had the sympathetic heart to feel it.

George Eliot's *Middlemarch* is not only about Dorothea and Casaubon; it is also about poverty, egoism, and philanthropy. The social duties of the Christian, she indicates, must be displayed in fellow feeling and philanthropy. In *Felix Holt*, Eliot says that 'a society, to be well off, must be made up chiefly of men who consider the general good as well as their own. "Common interest" must replace self-interest, and philanthropy must replace egotism.

In *Shirley*, Charlotte Bronte speaks the truth when she says "it is easy for those who are not hungry to palaver about the degradation of charity." She admonishes Shirley to disregard "the scruples of vain philosophy" and be philanthropic.

# CHAPTER 11

# MOTHERHOOD

To be a mother was a very "big number" as we are all conditioned to realise that, among Victorians as well as others, the treatment of one's mother by the hero or heroine of a novel was supposedly a guide to his character, for good or ill. The converse is the case in that even women who were shady human beings realised the character of their sons (usually their sons!) stood by them through thick and thin. Lady Carbury in *The Way We Live Now* is selfish, worldly, harsh with her daughter and in her world of writing hardly stops at anything—but all for her son, Felix. Roger Carbury thinks "Were she not foolishly weak, she would make up her mind to divide herself utterly from her son—this would bring him round. And when agony of want had tamed him he would be content to take bread and meat from her hand & would be humble" (chapter 7).

This has a ring of commonsense about it, but obviously Trollope feels she shows a redeeming side to her nature when she, everything weak and profligate about Felix having been revealed to her, still says: "It is no use telling me to leave him. I can't do that. I know him bad. I know that I have done much to make him what he is—but he is my child" (chapter 72). A different type of woman who is equally unlikeable in other fields but still has the "redeeming" feature of lingering maternal feelings is Mrs. Transome in *Felix Holt*. A much-loved son is coming home after fifteen years and we read that this woman, accustomed to exercise an iron will in other fields "had not the feminine tendency to seek influence through pathos; she had been used to rule through in virtue of this acknowledged superiority." She wanted to be the mother who would be consulted on all things. After all she had administered the lands while he was away—"Life would have little meaning for her if she was to be gently thrust aside as a harmless elderly woman" (chapter 1). She has doted on him as a boy and dreads any contretemps with him, but as George Eliot points out, "Mothers have a larger self than their maternity. There are wide spaces of their life which are not filled" (when the boys have gone away to College) "in praying for their boys, reading old letters and envying while blessing those who are attending to their shirt buttons" (chapter 8). She does feel, on his return, that the "The fatal threads" of mother-love are beginning to bind her again. But "She trembled under his kindness—the bitterness of this helpless bondage mingled itself with the elegancies of the dining-room and drawing-room which Harold had ordered with magical swiftess" (chapter 9). In other words, she knows that Harold is morally trying to bribe her with the sort of luxuries that are supposed to keep dominating women away from interfering with male pursuits.

The pages of Dickens are full of cosy mothers, no doubt of the type he felt his own mother was not. Mrs. Crisparkle in *Edmund Drood*, however, has far more reality in that, though deferring, apparently, to her son, the Canon, in public she does not really spoil him. She defends her ridiculous philosophical friend, regardless of Edmund's views; she still firmly takes Grace at table, despite her son's rank in the Church and ignores his kindly teasing about her eyesight, being very proud of her ability to read without spectacles. The first few pages of chapter 4 depict more easily than any individual quotations her staunch defence of Mr. Honeythunder; her tender affection for Edmund and her good-nature under teasing. Miss Mitford, perhaps because she is a spinster, but more likely because of her commonsense, implies it is very tedious to hear about children all the time. "One wonders what she could have talked about before she had children" (*Our Village*, "A Castle in the Air"). So evidently whether one liked children or not—and Miss Mitford often meets children in her walks whom she finds delightful—she feels mothers need to be a bit more than that. On the reverse side of that coin, Disraeli feels that Lady Marney is the better mother for being a clever woman. Speaking of Egremont he says, "He was fortunate in having a clever mother" (chapter 5). She is then described as worldly, polished, witty, eager to shine in her world. In many Victorian novels, this might culminate in the moral that she had little time for her children or they for her; but no, she was adored by her children, "for she was a mother most affectionate and true." Mrs. Woodward in Trollope's *Three Clerks* is not perhaps as clever or witty as Lady Marney, but she aspires to be a "modern" mother, no doubt, when she gives her daughters good advice "but did so, perhaps too much as an equal, too little as a parent." Later when Alaric seemingly woos Linda but with no real sincerity, Trollope apostrophises the mother in language that is sentimental but basically commonsensical. "Thou who art the kindest of others has it been well for thee to subject to such perils this poor weak dove of thine?" (chapter 3). Mrs. Woodward is not the usual matchmaking mother but being widowed young, she probably forgets that girlish emotions are not as controllable as a mature woman's. Apart from this criticism of her, Trollope has portrayed her as a delightful individual, maternity not shaping and wearing away her whole being.

Poverty and suffering, of course, often drove mothers to need to exert and demonstrate that side of their being to the momentary exclusion of all else. Mrs. Quiverful, when she hears that Slope has given back the wardenship to Mr. Harding, is a changed woman. "Within her bosom all the rage of the lioness, the rapacity of the hound—the deep despair of the mother" takes over and enables her to march straight off to the terrifying Mrs. Proudie (*Barchester Towers*, chapter 25). Mrs. Parker in *The Prime Minister* insists on an interview with Emily after Felix Lopez causes Septimus Parker to go bankrupt and cries, "If you had five children as hadn't bread you'd know as how it is I feel—I'd lie in a ditch and die if it was only for myself" (chapter 69). Mrs. Parker tends to be rather forthright in her language, otherwise so we find the note of pathos the more genuine for that. Suffering, on the other hand, tends to make Sylvia feel imprisoned by the very state of maternity, but maternity itself grows upon her by instinct. "She held the baby at her breast—she wished she were free from the duties and chains of matrimony, but the hold of the little mouth made her relax into gentleness and docility" (Gaskell: *Sylvia's Lovers*, chapter 33).

The prospect of a future daughter-in-law, of course, often brings out the more possessive side, as today, and according to their temperament, authors laugh or scold at this. The lack of other professional interests was the more specific difference between the centuries. Wolfe's mother cries out at her son's admiration for Miss Lowther. "We tend our children through fevers and measles whooping-cough and small-pox; we send them away to the Army and can't sleep for thinking; we break our heart for parting with 'em and having them at home for only a week in the year—after all our care, there comes a lass with a pair of bright eyes and away goes our boy and never gives a fig for us afterwards" (Thackeray: *Virginians*, chapter 24).

Wolfe, in fact, is a very good son, so Thackeray is teasing all mothers here. In this case the possible daughter-in-law would be considered "suitable," but in the case of Lucy in *Framley Parsonage*, although Lady Lufton is very fond of her as a person, she has never thought of her as even crossing her son's mind as a suitable partner. She has many feelings when she realises she must give in regarding the match, but among them is the awareness that she will no longer be a "Queen herself over the estate and, worse to come, Lucy's non-royal" relatives are to become her in-laws! (chapter 43). Incidentally, although Lady Lufton's love for her son was the paramount emotion she felt for him, we are told that, had he been dishonoured in any way, "she would have sunk to the grave in sorrow." Thus, in one sense, her critics were right when they said "Pride was her grinding-force" (chapter 43).

Another glance at Lady Carbury will emphasise this point. A simplistic view would be that Felix's mother was nearer to corruption herself than Lord Lufton's mother—but in actual fact, she was very ashamed of the standard he had sunk to, even if her own dubious standards were not much guide to him. Perhaps Lady Lufton might have felt differently about things if her son had deeply erred. Mrs. Fletcher, in *The Prime Minister*, is appalled by the conduct of Ferdinez Lopez but grudgingly admits that she has sympathy for Mr. Wharton but could not bring herself, like him, to see the man who disgraced his daughter. Her son teases her, saying, "You'd see him if he'd married a daughter of yours." She answers, "Never! If I had a child so lost to self-respect as that, I do not say I would not see her. Human nature might have prevailed. But I would not willingly put myself into conduct with one who had so degraded me and mine" (chapter 36). Evidently, in Trollope's world at any rate, there are varying degrees of maternal loyalty.

In another world, that of Mrs. Gaskell and of sharper tongues and great struggles, we see in Mrs. Wilson both aspects touched on in this paragraph: to be loyal to Jem against great odds comes easier to her than the giving up to a daughter-in-law. She never, for an instance, conceives of Jem being guilty of Carson's murder—not even when the specific ornamentation on the gun is pointed out. This is no blind loyalty. She knows the character of her son (chapter 19). Even though Mary Barton's evidence helps to save her son, Mrs. Wilson harps only on the duty of children to their parents above all others. Jem points out forcibly that "I can love you as dearly as ever, and Mary too, as much as man ever loved woman." Job had already pointed to to Jem that "A mother only gives up her son's heart inch by inch to his wife and then give it up with a grudge" and that she will not easily understand why he has to visit the sick girl in Liverpool (chapter 33). Only by gently reminding her of her own courting-days does he gradually win her round to a semblance of resignation to the situation. She has stood by him through very difficult times and she is a naturally fractious woman, partly due to an accident in younger days. So the solemn material blessing he finally wheedles from her is a tribute to her basic sincerity of an affection.

Mrs. Bretton in *Villette* has an astringent side towards her son, when he is an adult, although in many ways she could be said to have spoilt him as a child. "Don't be demonstrative, John, or I shall faint." She mocks when he says at the concert "Sensible, admirable old lady! You are better to me than ten wives yet" (chapter 20). Ginevre has been giving their party cool, quizzical glances and Mrs. Bretton's unperturbed comments on the insolent girl have pleased him. Maternity is very strong indeed in Mrs. Bretton, but it leaves enormous scope, nevertheless, for being her own woman.

Mrs. Yeobridge, in *The Return of the Native*, is also a person who gives a great affection to her son, but does not feel it good to show it either as regards her own character or his. She longs for him to do well in the diamond business and thinks he is lowering himself by becoming a teacher. However, many of his strong qualities come from her and he "could not fail to awaken a reciprocity in her through her feelings—disguise it as she might for his good" (chapter 2, Book 3). Hardy maintains that the love between mother and son was "indestructible" despite (or even because of) lack of demonstrativeness. Anyone listening to them would say "How cold they are to each other!" But this was not the true guide to their relationships. When Yeobridge says "her" in a fervid tone regarding Eustacia, Hardy remarks, "Hardly a maternal breast within the four seas could have helped being irritated at that ill-timed betrayal of feeling for another woman" (chapter 3, Book 3). It was "ill-timed" in that Mrs. Yeobridge has just been indicating to her son that she considers Eustacia unsuitable as a school-master's wife in that she is "Lazy and dissatisfied—and not as good a woman as one might desire." She makes this clear—and it is all true from her angle of life before Clym has shown his hand. She might not have spoken so condemningly if he had hinted, at first, to more than a passive fondness. The display of feelings may be anathema to these strong-charactered women, but their dislike of daughters-in-law, before and after the son's marriage, mirrors the very intensity they wish to hide.

The attitude towards maternity in the Victorian age is, of course, coloured by the tone of the speaker. Lucy has actively disliked Ginevre throughout the book, so it is not likely that she would ever seek for sincerity from her in the future. Once a mother, Ginevre writes reams about the whooping-cough and other ailments of her child, as if in agonies. But Lucy feels quite cynical about it all (Charlotte Bronte: *Villette*, chapter 40). Yet George Eliot, a very cynical woman in her own way, can see that Mrs. Vincy, normally self-indulgent and vain, neglects everything about herself because of her love for the sick Fred." Her brightness was all bedimmed — her senses dulled to the sights and sounds that used most to interest her (*Middlemarch*, chapter 26).

Likewise, Mrs. Holt, normally a harsh enough woman to judge, that is, from her manner and tone, could feel the old stirrings of maternity when she dealt with tiny children. "Like many women who appear to others to have a masculine decisiveness of tone, and to themselves to have a masculine force of mind, and who come into severe collision with sons arriving at the masterful stage, she had the maternal cord vibrating strongly towards all tiny children" (*Felix Holt*, chapter 43). This reflection on George Eliot's part comes about because Mrs. Holt is not naturally disposed to like Job being perhaps "patronised" by the rich visitors but now is moved that Dominic should pick up "the orphan child" and hold him on his arm for a while.

Mrs. Gaskell has a decisive, realistic tone of her own, too, realising that not all mothers are born to their role. Mrs. Thornton in *North and South* is a hard woman, but she still stays up yearning over her suffering son (chapter 50). When he tries to point that good or bad fortune comes equally from God, she shakes her head violently. "She would have nothing to do with religion just then." Her stern character is only moved when John points out that any truly religious principles he has imbided came from her in his childhood — when she had far worse troubles than now. She bitterly indicates that those troubles were her troubles, but it is harder to see her son, a good man, humiliated. She has come a long way from Mrs. Thornton who sat brooding bitterly on all the pride of place she would have to yield to a future daughter-in-law and then savagely cursed Margaret when she hears she has refused John. Another aspect, this time of indirect motherhood, is the compassionate way each poor woman takes a child of Mrs. Boucher's when her husband is drowned. "It was who could do most, and the children are sure of a bellyful today, and of kindness too" (*North and South*, chapter 36).

Poor Mrs. Rudge is in a very difficult position because her seemingly strong adult son is simple, but she does not "baby" him if at all possible to prevent so humiliating him—but when he is in prison, her struggles become even more realistic as she first reads to him to keep up his spirits and then her fortitude collapses and she "falls upon his neck," when she finally realises there is to be no reprieve for him from the gallows (chapter 76). The poor young man "wonders at her anguish" as he can only see glory in his fate and he is, as we know, to be finally rescued, but this does not make Mrs. Rudge the less pitiful in her suddenly relaxed strength of character.

It is refreshing, of course, to see the human face of the often deified Victorian maternal qualities. In *The Kellys and the O'Kelleys*, we can see that Mrs. O'Kelly is basically a doting mother, but she likes this fact to be recognised and, alas, like many mothers even today, more consideration is given to the son than the daughters. When she expresses horror that she is to be dragged into legal trouble on behalf of her son, Martin knows that "Much of her lamentation—was a laudable wish to appear a martyr to the wishes of her children" (chapter 20). In the case of the girls, though she has married off one with a good "portion," she still expects her remaining daughters "while sharing their mother's home to share her labours and they were not allowed to be too proud to cut off pennyworths of tobacco and mix dandies of snuff" for the customers, although they keep two servants in the house (chapter 1).

So it is not surprising to read, at the end of the novel, that although Martin has married Anty and a fortune and Mrs. Kelly is too proud to do more than visit at the big house, though they beg her to live there, the girls remark that though they may take "turn about" in the "nasty old place" (meaning their mother's inn), Meg, for one, remarks, "Fancy coming down here, Matilda, to the tobacco and sugar, after living up there for a month or two—and it's only mother's whims, for she doesn't want the shop."

# CHAPTER 12

# FAMILY LIFE

It is in the family circle that we often see girls or young women as their true, uncurbed selves — whether it be in an outspoken attitude towards their brothers or in a headstrong exchange with their mothers. The latter, of course, is not encouraged by the author among "good" girls. On the other hand, a weak mother might sometimes be seen as in need of such toughening by the book's creator! Fathers, of course, were a different proposition, but here again if a daughter had spirit, she might be allowed to resist an over-dominating papa. Simply because they are not in the public eye, girls in family life are the nearest we often see to natural uninhibited human beings even among the most conservative authors.

Mary Garth, we are told, affectionately was "a little hoyden" as a child (Eliot: *Middlemarch*, chapter 23, Book 3) and Rosamund in the same book speaks extremely naturally to her brother at home. "Really, Fred, if you must have hot things for breakfast, I wish you would come down earlier. You can get up at six o'clock to go hunting; I cannot understand why you find it so difficult to get up on other mornings." Rosy is far from being a likeable young lady, but our sympathies must be with her when she asks Fred sarcastically what he would think if she came down two hours late and ordered a grilled bone, only to be given the answer that he would think her "an uncommonly fast young lady!" She echoes the cry of sisters through the centuries as she says "I cannot see why brothers are to make themselves any more disagreeable than sisters" (chapter 11, Book 1).

To turn to another female writer since I suppose women in the nineteenth century had both more sympathy for girlhood freedom and yet in some ways were more censorious if it took a "spoilt" form; Lizzie in *Our Village* is a very distinctive child who is obviously going to be an equally individual adult." A child of three according to the register, but six in size and strength and intellect, in power and self-will. The silent talk to her, the grave romp with her—her chief attraction lies in her exceeding power of loving and her firm reliance on the love and indulgence of others." The latter part of this description might merely add up to charm and affection, but we hear she can "manage even her schoolmistress" and has something of the character of Napoleon (chapter 1). Young Lizzie is the village cabinet maker's child, so Miss Mitford is not marking out for future heroine role the indulged squire's daughter—but it does make the modern readers wonder why such will-power and individualism are less desired in adult maidens both in Victorian literature and life.

In *Rachel Raye*, we see that girls can tyrannise over their mothers even when it is not called for (i.e., as suggested in the first paragraph, when a weak mother needs help to resist bullying elsewhere in the family). He points out ironically that, once that daughter becomes a visitor only, she loses her hold! Mrs. Ray has always been afraid of Dorothea, her eldest, but when Dolly is considering marriage a second time, she tries to lord it on future visits but her grip is gone. Mrs. Ray now becomes afraid of her younger daughter but in a different way. "No visitor can hold such dominion there may be held as a domestic tyrant present at all meals, and claiming an ascendancy in all conversations" (chapter 23). But Rachel is not unpleasant like her sister; she just sternly refuses to discuss Luke Rowan and her mother feels a terrible guilt as she had refused his entry to the cottage—yet knows her daughter is grieving deeply. Rachel is no Marianne Dashley, however. She may be pining and, quite naturally, does not wish Luke's departure, but she certainly partakes astringently enough in family life when she says, apropos of her sister's new intended, "she'll never give up her money and he'll never marry her unless she does."

Women within the family circle are often given a kind of dutch courage in order to demonstrate their seeming or genuine power over their husbands. In Trollope's *Three Clerks*, we are told that women often know more of their husbands' business affairs even when the latter imagine they kept from them. "The partner of one's bed and board—cannot but have the means of guessing the thoughts which occupy her companion's mind and occasionally darken his brow" (chapter 17). In the same way, the mother and daughter in the Tappitt family are not prepared to stand too much from Mrs. Tappitt despite the "duty" Victorian women had instilled into them to "obey." "She knew her duty and she could stand a great deal. But there were some things she couldn't stand and some things that weren't her duty" (chapter 22).

The chapter is in fact headed "Domestic Politics at the Brewery" and one cannot pretend that Mrs. Tappitt or her daughters are very pleasant people, but enough is enough and near-bankruptcy is hardly a thing to be kept from one's family until the last moment! Mr. Tappitt can in fact, if he swallows his pride, retire with "a very handsome income," but that has not been made very clear to the female members of his family at this juncture! Mrs. Grantly is again and again shown, in private, as admonishing or being highly sarcastic towards the awesome Archdeacon before whom, in public, she appears humble and decorous.

Chapters 2 and 8 of *The Warden* particularly illustrate this, especially in the latter when the Archdeacon starts to boast that once Sir Abraham Haphazard helps him reach the "bench of Bishops" the family fortunes will flow better than ever. "Oh, Sir Abraham won't get Eleanor a husband; Sir Abraham won't get papa another income when he has been worried out of the hospital—while you and Sir Abraham are fighting, papa will lose his preferment and what will you do then with him and Eleanor on your hands?" Trollope comments wryly that the Archdeacon had his "submissive" role to play in the dressing-room, when his wife was in hot defence of her sister's right to happiness and "The wise and talented lady too well knew the man to whom her lot for life was bound to stretch her authority beyond the point at which it would be borne." At least, we have already heard, as early as chapter 2, that "it arose that our archdeacon listened to the counsels of his wife, though he considered himself entitled to give counsel to every other being whom he met"!

It is hard to see women who are recognized in society as witty intellectuals and considerably more intelligent than their husbands giving into those domestic tyrants for family peace, even though in the outer world they are not particularly weak-willed women. Lady Arabella Marnay in *Sybil* "—had excellent sense and possessed many admirable qualities," but "she yielded without a struggle to the arbitrary will and unreasonable caprice of a husband who was hardly her equal in intellect and far her inferior in all the genial qualities of our nature." She had fought at the beginning and in the early days of their marriage, after much remonstration had been "invisible for days, plunged in remorseful reveries." But his sheer selfish will "broke her in" at last (Disraeli: *Sybil*, chapter 6). Yet Lord Marnay did not consider himself cruel: he merely thought her earlier behavior due to a girlish misunderstanding of what marriage was all about and "ignorant of his wise authority." Yet in other homes, in different circles an unpleasant dominating man, disliked by everybody, can be ruled by an otherwise amenable wife. In *Shirley* we are informed that Mr. Sympson, the very man who swears at the strong-willed heroine in such foul language that she turns white and nearly faints, will be ultimately prevented by his wife from suing Louis or Shirley as he childishly threatens when he sees Fieldhead is not coming in to his hands. "I know his wife, over whom he tyrannises in trifles, guides him in matters of importance" (chapter 36).

An interesting aspect of family life—and one repeated today among proud mothers, especially if widows, is in Mrs. Thornton's totally different manner towards her son and her daughter. She dotes on John but is too proud to show it; she is a little ashamed of Fanny's simplicity but salves her conscience by being very affectionate towards her. "She never called her son any name but John; "love" and "dear" and such like terms were reserved for Fanny," but earlier one reads "The very daringness with which mother and son spoke out unpalatable truths, the one to the other, showed a reliance on the firm centre of each other souls" (*North and South* chapter 12). Emily Wharton in *The Prime Minster* is regarded in her family home as "rather a strong-minded young woman," so this makes it doubly sad as her marriage breaks her spirit. She retains enough of this to bear the loss of her baby better when she "tells herself that it is better to be robbed of her treasure—with such a father as she had given him" (chapter 49). The lively girl used to ruling in the home does fight it out at the beginning, but Victorian ideas of duty to husbands must—at least on the surface prevail.

In *The Kellys and the O'Kellys*, we see some very natural exchanges in both the high-ranking group and the low-ranking. The Kelly girls who are prepared to be kind when nursing others are apt to become petulant, when they are ill themselves. "When ill they felt they had a right to complain; to exact and to be attended to; they had been used to it from each other and thought it an incidental part of the business" (chapter 24).

Mrs. Armstrong has a conversation with her family that rings very true today although, having been brought up as a "lady," she is ashamed of Lord Bellindine overhearing her scolding. Now, Greg, "if you leave your meat that way, I'll have it put by for you and you shall have nothing but potatoes till it's ate." To this the boy spiritedly replies, "Why,

Mother, it's nothing but tallow; look here; you gave me all the outside part." There then follows an example of tale-bearing regarding the stealing of some jam, which hints little of Victorian repression, despite the mother's appearance of acting fiercely (chapter 26).

To return to the Kellys. Mrs. Kelly cannot be prevailed upon to live in the Big House when Martin and Anty get married for the most understandable reasons, but they are expressed in such a way that we, once again, can see women can be themselves in family life: especially strong-willed widows. She wouldn't think of being a trouble to young folks—she had always been mistress in her own house, and mostly master, too, thank God, and she meant to be so still, and that poor as the place was she meant to call it her own—she had always lived in a place where money was made, and she didn't see the sense of going, in her old age to a place where the only work was how to spend it"! (Final chapter).

Again, although Mrs. Varden's personality in *Barnaby Rudge* may be much exaggerated in her display of "temperaments," she does at least show that women could get away with a great deal in the home. There is no underdog about her nor is she a real shrew at all. The neighbours know she would be loyal to her husband in adversity, as she turns out to be, realising, in fact, that she has behaved hitherto like a spoilt wilful child rather than the mature woman she basically can be. "Divers wise men and matrons on friendly terms with the locksmith and his family went so far as to assert that a tumble down—the world's ladder would be the making of her" and could hardly fail to render her one of the most agreeable companions in existence (Dickens: *Barnaby Rudge*, chapter 6 and 7).

# CHAPTER 13

# CLASS DISTINCTION AMONG WOMEN

I will be differentiating here between a woman's attitude towards men who might me marriageable, if the class-barrier can be surmounted and the barrier between women themselves, which is often surmountable if the two women concerned have other things in common.

To take a rather absurd example of the first relationship (for after all the hero is a gentleman by any standard), Geraldine's reflection in *The Indiscretion of an Heiress.*" Egbert and Geraldine "realise simultaneously" the gap between them when they discuss how far the tower is from Westcombe when she assumes the distance would be covered by driving and he calculates it according to *walking*. "It was the horrid thought of their differing positions and their contrasting habits which could not be reconciled" (chapter 6). In a different milieu, we see Georgiana Longstaffe—described earlier as having the sharpest tongue and the strongest head of the family—drawing the line with the nouveau riche whose wealth derives, she considers, from dishonest means. "No one knows who they are nor where they come from, nor what they'll turn to" (Trollope: *The Way We Live Now*, chapter 13). Ironically, of course having spent all her father's money quite recklessly when she could, she is to allow herself to become engaged to a seemingly "shady" business man, when her father's money runs out!

To turn to women relating class-wise to women, Lady Lufton in *Framley Parsonage* when thinking about Lucy Robarts considers "she has shown talent, good temper and sound judgment but then there has been no quiet, no repose about her—dignified reticence: of this poor Lucy has none" (Trollope: *Framley Parsonage*, chapter 35). However it turns out that although her concept of a Society lady is one of forever unbroken calm, Trollope mischievously adds that Lucy lacks money and birth, "which was greater evil"! When Lucy does, in fact, become engaged to Lord Lufton, we read with amazement that Mrs. Crawley, who had clung to Lucy during her sickness and Lucy's skilled nursing, is shattered to think of being ministered by a future peeress. Her manner alters completely, although one reads that she herself was a "lady" before her marriage and family brought her to great poverty. Lucy senses this and says, "It must make no difference, you know, between you and me. Promise me that it will make no difference." The promise is made, but the author remarks that "it was not possible that such a promise should be kept" (chapter 46). Such were Victorian mores!

"Propriety" was held in greater respect in the higher ranks as one supposes that working women would hardly need to "whisper" the words "Thief," "Robber," "Swindler" regarding Lizzie Eustace when they felt it so strongly as the Fawns did in *The Eustace Diamonds* (chapter 60). Even here, however, a generation gap must have been felt within one's own class as Lady Fawn is very upset that ladies are so changed that her own daughter, Mrs. Hittaway, can bring Andy Gowan to her mother to give express details of Lizzie and Frank kissing among the Scottish rocks (glad as she is of such evidence!). She feels "most assuredly she could not have brought an Andy Gowan to her mother to tell such tales, in their joint presence as this man told" (Trollope: *Eustage Diamonds*, chapter 60).

In the matter of servants and ladies, of course, few of the former thought of crossing the "gap"—warm-heartedness as to an inferior, yes, to be expected from a virtuous heroine, but a search for equality rarely arose. A tentative struggle in this direction is made by the tender-spirited Laura when Pendonnis insults the cook for giving his arm to a lady (Blanche Amory) by addressing him loudly by his rank. Laura points out, "Foreigners may be more susceptible than we are and have different manners. If you hurt a poor man's feelings, I am sure you would be the first to ask his pardon" (*Pendennis*, chapter 37).

In *The Hand of Ethelberta*, Mrs. Malove points out to Picotee that town servants are not the same as country ones. "We are all independent here; no slavery for us: it is not the same as it is in the country, where servants are considered to be of different bone and blood from their employers, and to have no eye for anything but their work." Menlove, the housekeeper, has already pointed out to Picotee rather sarcastically that her desire to see the "Company" is misplaced as "They are not much to see, you know" (chapter 29). It has to be remembered, of course, that Picotee's own father is working as butler in this same household and is "serenely happy and comfortable" in that position, much as

his other daughter Ethelberta, busy grooming herself for marriage with
at least an earl, would rather see him as "Caretaker at some provincial
library, country stationer, registrar of births and deaths—"anything that
would appear more respectable! (chapter 28). To say nothing that Mr.
Chickerel has already told Ethelberta in the same chapter that he would
rather see her dead than Lord Mountclere's wife "or the wife of anyone
like him."

Ethelberta, of course, is in a difficult position, in that she has been
left a small fortune by her employer. This and her looks give her an
entreé into high society but only if she covers up her antecedents! Her
earlier marriage to her employer's son had also done so, as she quite
frankly says to her father, "My marriage being so secret made it it easy
to cut off all traces unless someone has made it a special business to
search for them." Poor Ethelberta, she is in a real muddle as she is
deeply devoted to her father and wants him to live with her and be
cared for—but as he points out, "I have been in service now for more
than seven and thirty years. It is an honourable calling and why should
you maintain me because an old woman left you her house and a few
sticks of furniture. If she had left you any money, it would be different,
but as you have to work for every penny you get, I cannot think of it."
Again, one might say "poor Lady Petherwin" would hardly like the home
she treasured to be called "A few sticks." But perhaps all her memory
deserved in view of the hauteur with which she had treated her daughter-
in-law and after her son's early death the casual manner in which she
treated Ethelberta as a companion despite the fact that in the first
chapter we read that Ethelberta had earlier "become teacher in a school,
was praised by examiners—and touched up by accomplishments." The
later two or three years in a finishing school at Bonn, one presumes,
was done at her mother-in-law's expense for the latter's benefit to give
her a suitable "air" for a family connection.

To return directly to the servant-mistress theme: when Mrs. Don-
castle discovers at last that Ethelberta is the daughter of her own butler,
she is more horrified than if he had been "The vilest Antipodean miscre-
ant or murderer"! (chapter 42). This despite the fact that she has always
considered Ethelberta a perfect lady and very accomplished. Hardy drily
points out that remoteness of criminality would hardly have shook her
so much as the nearness of low-caste!

Mind you, where does Hardy himself stand in all this? Leaving
aside his inherent love of the twisted, eccentric plot, his feeling for social

equality seems merely to extend to thinking that a good education and polished manners should outweigh ancestry or money, but he is not terribly concerned that it doesn't do so. With a male character, such as Jude, it appears to be different—but then marriagability with higher rank is not involved, but equality with one's own sex.

In *Barchester Towers* (chapter 39, volume 12), the creation of the Lookalofts seems to indicate a view on Trollope's part that women are more snobbish than men. Mrs. Lookaloft has changed "Barleystub" Farm to "Rosebank," whereas we gather Mr. Lookaloft is content just to own as much land and pay his rent as regularly as Mr. Greenacre—in the vestry. Yet, Trollope seems to contradict this when Fanny in "The Kellys and the O'Kellys" tells Selina that love of rank is ridiculous if it goes before genuine feelings (chapter 28). On the other hand, this is a woman discussing feelings for a man rather than the comparative rank of her own sex. Fanny is fond enough of Selina, but she retorts strongly, "You who think more of your position as an earl's daughter—an aristocrat, than of your nature as a woman!" Fanny is poor but of good breeding; Lord Ballintine, her suitor is more exalted, but to Selina and her father too feckless for marriage. So "Rank" is rather too tenuous a concept for either woman to bring into the argument, but as it is serious to them, one can at least see that Fanny's point of view is more admirable. As one would expect from the pen of Disraeli, he puts great scorn upon the lips of Mr. Millbank when he describes to Coningsby why Lord Monmouth did not consider Coningsby's mother good enough to unite with Monmouth's own "Because they were not noble, because they could trace no mystified descent from a spoiling invader or the sacriligious minion of some spoliating despot, their daughter was barred from the family which should have exalted to receiver her" (chapter 8, Book 7). Strong stuff, but, alas the women in his novels do not express themselves so strongly, though doubtless feeling as much. In the same vein, Tom Pinch, in *Martin Chuzzlewit* feels very strongly on his sister's behalf, telling her employer, "When you place her at a disadvantage to every servant in your house, how can you suppose she is not in a tenfold worse position in reference to your daughters?" (chapter 36). Again, one supposes Ruth notices and feels deeply the humiliations of being a governess but, after all, until her brother comes to "rescue" her, she has to earn her bread and butter.

Women authors with such sensitivity to the sufferings of the poor as Mrs. Gaskell would, one supposes, have a feeling that natural worth surmounts all class—and to a certain extent that is true. Mary Barton is a far more interesting heroine than many to be in nineteenth-century literature and her flirtatious weakness is never blamed on social background (Harry Carson's dazzling charm, not his wealth attracts her). Ruth is considered by Elizabeth Gaskell to be, "although not altogether a lady by birth and education," "able to be placed among the highest in the land, and would have been taken by the most critical judge as their equal although ignorant of their conventional etiquette" ("Ruth", chapter 19). Yet who are these highest in the land? Certainly the father of her child is hardly a prime example. He abandons her, not because he finds her boring as does Dahlia's lover, in *Rhoda Fleming*, but mainly because his mother represents her as unfit for decent society! To be fair her total ascent to a lady has evidently, in the quotation already given, been achieved by spiritual regeneration and assimilating the manners and ways of the kind and well-educated Bensons who would have a hearty contempt for the Harry Bellinghams of this world.

Margaret in *North and South* shows no class-consciousness when she earnestly begs Higgins not to go to the South to look for work, desperate as he is, as he has no idea of the painful toil involved. Hard as a labouring man's day is in the industrial North, he cannot conceive of how much worse it would be. "They labour on from day to day, in the great solitude of steaming fields—never speaking or lifting up their poor, bent, downcast heads. The hard spade-work robs their brains of life—what would be peace to them, would be eternal fretting to you" (chapter 37).

Charlotte Bronte's Shirley shows a similar naturalness in conversing with the gardener William. She and Caroline "Both liked William; it was their delight to lend him books, to give him plants; and they preferred his conversation far above that of many coarse, hard, pretentious people, immeasurably above him in station" (chapter 18). For those unfamiliar with Shirley's character, this might read as condescension, but true sincerity is the keynote of her character. For those still unconvinced, one has but to read the author's steely sarcasm in the chapter heading, "In which certain low characters are introduced, which the genteel reader is recommended to skip!"

To return to *Mary Barton*: Mrs. Gaskell invites the reader irritated by her sixteen-year-old flights of fancy to consider "What are the silly fancies of sixteen years in any class and underall circumstances?" (chapter 3). She also points out that Mrs. Carson lacks the education to "value the resources of wealth and leisure." She has headaches, which might have been cured if "She could rub tables, shake carpets and go out in the fresh morning air," i.e., "Take the work of one of her housemaids for a week" (chapter 18).

In *Sylvia's Lovers*, the warden's wife and daughters mean well to Philip, even suggesting the free use of the cottage for him. Mrs. Gaskell, however, points out the warden himself questions him "with kindly inquisitiveness, as the rich do question the poor." Nevertheless the young Miss Pennington instinctively wishes to be genuinely kind (chapter 41).

George Eliot as one might assume is more interested in intelligence than class, but when certain elegances and fastidiousness are observed in Esther (*Felix Holt*) she seems to need to reassure the reader that they are basically the result of her father's good "birth" despite his current poverty. Before she goes to Transome Court and sees the emptiness of life there, she spends a great deal of her life dreaming about high life. "No one who has not, like Esther, a strong natural prompting towards such things, and has at the same time suffered the opposite condition, can understand how these minor accidents of rank which please the fastidious sense can preoccupy the imagination" (chapter 38). Because she is in love with a radical, because other deep sufferings strengthen her character, she gives up the chance of a fortune and all "refinements," but somehow the authoress has still worked in her natural right to be a "lady"! Turning to another female writer, Miss Mitford is in general unperturbed by "the rich man in his castle, the poor man at his gate" concept of her day, but yet her most lively and interesting characters are often of very low origins and she sighs over her rich young friend who would be a much better writer "if she were not a person of great beauty and a woman of fortune. That is to say, if she were prompted by either of those stimuli, want of money or want of admiration to take due pains—she would inevitably become a clever writer" ("The Shaw" from *Our Village*; see author's footnote on a letter received from a friend).

There are, of course, the usual English castes within castes even among some of the so-called working classes in nineteenth-century literature. Mrs. Billikins in *Edwin Drood*, although a caricature, is still obviously a sensible, worthwhile woman in her own right, but at the mere thought that Miss Twinkleton might be patronising her, she becomes foolish and only "communicates" with that lady through Rosa. Miss Twinkleton in her own affected manner does not hesitate to use the same means. The latter asks the landlady through Rosa, "Perhaps, my love, you could tell the person of the house whether she can procure us a lamb's fry!" The haughty answer being, "If you were better accustomed to butcher's meat, Miss, you would not entertain the idea—Try a little invention, Miss, use yourself to 'ousekeeping a bit" (chapter 22). That Mrs. Billikin is very honest and therefore admirable in Dickens' eyes is evident in her earlier account of her rooms, stressing that her bedroom floors are not "firm" in the ordinary sense because the gas fitter himself allowed he would have to go right under the joists to make a firm job and it were not worth the outlay as a yearly tenant so to do." However she adds that any house will rattle at that elevation in really galey weather, but it would happen "Do you worst or best." No rooms are to be taken under false pretences here! (chapter 22, ibid).

Although Ruby Ruggles in *The Way We Live Now* despises John Crumb for his roughness and has escaped to London because of his attentions, she is horrified to think that he should even hear of her "going into Service," with which her aunt threatens her if she continues to see Felix Carbury secretly. Yet she has been working as hard as any servant at her aunt's lodging and frequently for worse hours! (chapter 80).

# CHAPTER 14

# WOMEN'S ABILITY TO COPE WITH POVERTY

There are two aspects to this subject: the day by day struggle of the genuinely poor—and within that scope how much resentment or cheerful acceptance was involved—and the sudden descent of women of middle class to comparative poverty and, similarly their reactions thereto.

John McVeagh in his "Elizabeth Gaskell" (*Profiles in Literature,* chapter 1) speaks of "The realistic squalor described among the urban proletariat" and goes on to quote from *Mary Barton,* chapter 10. Certainly the squalor is there—the house stripped of its ornaments because the money they brought was required for the "far sterner necessities of food." Naturally Mrs. Gaskell is making social criticism (as the Critic's article is headed), but, as she is also extremely interested in the maturing of Mary's character, something else must be emerging from the remark that follows: "The smart tea-caddy, long and carefully kept, went for bread for her father. He did not ask for it, he did not complain but she saw hunger in his shrunk-look. The blanket went because it was summertime and Mary fancied the fund they made would last till better times came round." Of course, such things should not have been, but Mary is at least at a very young age showing an effort not to be merely feckless and uncaring.

By contrast, Sylvia in *Sylvia's Lovers* copes but suffers emotionally. She struggles and struggles with the landwork to please her mother who could not bear to leave Haytersbank, but as she says to old Kester, "It would take two pair of men's hands to keep the land as Master Hall likes it" (chapter 28). She could leave the place and find other work if it wasn't for her mother's grief. So she finally decides to marry Philip much against her better judgment. This will not enable her to live in the old home, but Philip can't keep mother in comfort for the rest of her days."

The washerwoman in *Our Village* is not desperately poor, but she has had to struggle and is a fine, independent character, even though only a thumbnail sketch is given of her. Her home is described as "A little ruinous cottage, whitewashed once, and now in a sad state of betweenity, where dangling stockings and shirts, drying in a neglected garden, give signal of a washerwoman." No children are spoken of and her husband lives ten miles off working as gardener for a big house. If Mrs. Adams prefers, therefore, to spend her hard earnings on "green tea, gin and snuff," rather than in repairing her cottage, we gather Miss Mitford feels "good luck to her!"

The whole chapter entitled "Rachel" in Dicken's *Hard Times* (chapter 13) is very moving in that Rachael is quietly content in her poverty though obviously long ago saddened and still overshadowed by her love for Stephen. Stephen even calls her an "Angel" because of her care for her "fallen" friend, but she says, "Angels are not like me. Between them and a working woman full of faults there is a deep gulf fixed." Stephen's wife, on whom Rachael is keeping an eye, has taken to drink and prostitution, and much as Stephen now shrinks from her, one feels that Dickens thinks of the iniquities of Coketown and the Gradgrinds of this life whose masterdom led to poverty with which some could cope and some not but which was still iniquitous. Poverty was unacceptable to Dickens, no doubt, because he had been much humiliated by it as a child. Nevertheless, heroic women are more acceptable to him if they are calm and content in the grip of poverty. Bitterness and resentment are best left to men or to authors!

Coping with poverty when one has "come down in the world" or when one marries someone from a different income group is faced in varying ways. Mrs. Parker in *The Prime Minister* can cope with Sexty's gambling, but she says to Emily that she could not "sit as you are sitting" if she knew that her husband had ruined another man. Emily has made the excuse that she does not understand her husband's affairs and poor Mrs. Parker cries out: "Don't you feel no shame? Because you have got things comfortable here—you don't care, though my children were starving in the gutter—as they will do." Of course Emily does care and fetches what little money Felix allows her. Sexty has been a worthless character and perhaps, when he was affluent, Mrs. Parker has looked the other way if she suspected something shady. But Felix is heartless, she knows it, and fights as best she can for her children even when the formidable Mrs. Wharton appears on the scene (chapter 55).

From a different background, the gently brought-up Gertrude in Trollope's *The Three Clerks* is able to face poverty in Australia. "Through poverty, scorn, and bad repute under the privations of a hard life—Gertrude was able to remain true to her marriage vows" 48). Single women have their problems of unknown poverty to face with varying attitudes also. *Diana of the Crossways* could have called upon her husband or her close friend Emma for money but prefers her shabby lodgings because "I can eat when I want, walk, work—and I am working! My legs, my pen, demand it!" (chapter 13).

Modern readers may well say "Well, she could go back to her husband," if poverty really pushed her, or she had the hope of making money one day. The fact remains that voluntary poverty was a very independent concept in the nineteenth-century for a young woman. The poetess whom Pendennis meets is not ashamed to travel alone on an omnibus, even though she trails straw from its floor on the bottom of her dress, into the comparatively snobbish gathering, "what a comfort it was to get a ride all the way from Brompton." No one laughs at this speech, comments Pen, "it was uttered so simply" (Thackeray: *Pendennis*, chapter 34).

In the same book, we hear from the author that, fiendish as The Campaigner is in general, when she is staying in Boulogne with her daughter and son-in-law, she manages to make their lodgings presentable with very little money "Homely, pretty, and comfortable." Her timid, indecisive daughter did not really know how to "manage," even if this were due to her mother's over-domination (Thackeray: *Newcomes*, chapter 72). The Campaigner hasn't much taste, apparently. Some of the ornaments are "such fugitive gimcrack things as they brought away with them," but this is irrelevant as she can, at least make something out of nothing. In a different type of situation, Ethelberta is extremely resourceful in planning a lodging house, with all her family in useful positions, while she herself is a breadwinner in another field, as "The Storyteller," "Hand of Ethelberta," (chapter 15). Admittedly all her family have "positions" already, but this will give them some measure of independence and her mother more leisure. The foolish girl is going to hide the fact that these people are related to her when mixing herself with Society, but at least, apart from her father who is adamant in his own dignity as butler, she has brought her family together. "I have thought over every possible way of combining the dignified social position I must maintain to make my story-telling attractive, with my absolute lack of money and I can see no other way." When Mr. Redworth leaves it too long to propose to Diana, because he feels a man should provide a woman with comforts in her new home, Emma, not liking to break it to him outright that she has that very morning had a note from Diana to say she is married to Warwick, remarks, "Women are not really puppets. They are not so excessively luxurious. It is good for young women, in the early days of marriage to rough it a little" (chapter 5).

Q. D. Leavis, speaking of the final meeting of Estella and Pip (in the published ending, not the alternative one, which he does not prefer) remarks: "Estella is now saddened, a poor widow, has passed through the distasteful hands of Drummle and has nothing left but the site of Satis House" (chapter 6, *Dickens the Novelist*). Leavis contends that she has gone through an experience comparable with Pip's humiliations and gradual self-knowledge so that her new, relative "poverty" helps to bring them together. A little real life is to bring Disraeli's Sybil more in touch with her tenderness for the truly poor. Yet, her father wants her permanently in the cloister because, he says to Gerard, "For the married woman of our class in the present condition of our country, is a lease of woes, slaves and the slaves of slaves!" (*Sybil*, chapter 16, Book 2).

Had Sybil have a true vocation to convent life, things would be different. But we see her—and even then but spasmodically—at her most natural in the "World." No doubt she will get more opportunity to help the underprivileged when she eventually reaches wealth through an extraordinary twist of plot, but coping with poverty and among the poor is her least puppet-like role. Loyalty to a husband sometimes brings out a quiet strength in sudden emergencies.

In *Framley Parsonage*, Fanny has been brought up in a sheltered manner and is now used to the dignity of a parson's wife. Yet, when the bailiffs are in the yard, thanks to Mark's gambling, she feels no shame—expressing only love for her husband sitting disconsolate in his study" . . . "who is to be true to you if I am not?" (Trollope: *Framley Parsonage*, chapter 44). This does not mean, of course, that she has not rebuked him in a frank manner in the course of events leading up to this day! Mark, a very likeable young man, appears completely incapable of even meeting the bailiffs or of planning the rest of his life. Practicality in women and great common-sense is hereby illustrated.

Timid, helpless Annette in *Felix Holt* can shed her apathy when it is question of aiding her baby. "I have sold some of the books to make money and I have looked into the shops where they sell caps and bonnets and pretty things and I could do all that and get more money to keep us" (chapter 6). In the same way, the necessity to nurse Mr. Lyon takes her mind off total proccupation with the baby and the brooding torpor that had descended on her after the long search for her dead husband. Her one skill is the aforementioned making of pretty things, and she is at last able to realise that she could gain some sort of income were she to do this for money.

To sum up: women are admired for coping within the circles of the poor, but, in a way, it is taken for granted that they are used to it. Of course, it is admirable if they are cheerful and show fortitude about it. Those who come down in the world have less, to modern eyes, to bear. Yet, they seem to touch the hearts of their creators more. There are striking exceptions, naturally. It is unlikely that anyone will move us more than the suffering Margaret in *Mary Barton*, not even Mrs. Wilson despite her whining tendencies. In fact, it isn't that less compassion is shown to the real poor. It is just that a certain tender empathy will steal over a middle-class writer should someone from a similar background begin to show deprivation.

The culture of poverty presents a picture that indicates a qualitative difference in beliefs and attitudes of male and female writers in nineteenth-century England. There was a general agreement that to be impoverished is to be an alienated being and to grow up in a culture that is radically different from the one that dominates the society as a whole. Many writers saw the culture of poverty as a reaction of the alienated poor to their deplorable position in a class-stratified and individualistic society. One of the characteristics of the poor is the feeling of powerlessness and resignation, which is always associated with the awareness of a lack of effective social participation and integration.

The Industrial Revolution affected the lives of all people in England. Some of its effects were only short-lived. It was the changeover from hand to factory working that bore most heavily upon the working population. Wages were low, hours of work were long, machinery was unprotected, accidents were frequent, and there was no compensation for those injured. Little children aged five to seven were employed for the same long hours as the adults. Women, too, worked long hours and had no time to look after their homes. In many areas, especially in Yorkshire, East Anglia, and the West Country, there was much unemployment and poverty.

Utilitarian writers and philosophers attributed poverty to "the law of nature." Thomas Malthus, Jeremy Bentham, and Herbert Spencer show no sympathy for the poor. They regard poverty as a consequence of personal failings. They were fanatical believers in free enterprise and in class stratification of society.

In the first half of the nineteenth-century, an increasing number of male and female writers wrote about the deplorable condition of the poor and stirred up public opinion. Thomas Carlyle wrote critically of "the liberty to die by starvation." Elizabeth Barrett Browning wrote in *The Cry of Children:* "They never see the sunshine. . . . They look up with their pale and sunken faces, And their look is dread to see. . . ." In *Michael Armstrong*, Trollope's mother Frances gives a melodramatic account of child labour in the factories and in *Jessie Phillips* attacks the Poor Law of 1834, like Dickens in *Oliver Twist*. In 1841 Charlotte E. Tonna exposed the miseries of the rural poor in her work *Helen Fleetwood*.

Describing the conditions in the southwest of England as they existed in 1821, William Cobbett was so disappointed that he longed for a return to the past. In *Rural Rides* he writes: "The labourers along here seem very poor indeed. A group of women labourers presented an assemblage of rags I never saw before, many of whom are common beggars. There were some very pretty girls but as ragged as colts and as pale as ashes. Their dwellings are little better than pig-beds."

The report of a Royal Commission in 1841, appointed to investigate the condition in the coal-mining industry, shocked all people in England with its revelation of the brutality that existed in mines. This revelation was reflected immediately in English literature, including Elizabeth Gaskell's *Mary Barton* and Benjamin Disraeli's *Sybil*. During the remainder of the nineteenth century, there was a steady stream of criticism directed against egoistic utilitarianism and unregulated industrialism. In *Past and Present*, Thomas Carlyle blames "competition" and "laissez-faire or free trade" for the phenomenon of poverty in England. In spite of England's "plethoric wealth," he says, "England is dying of inanition."

In *Hard Times* (1854), Dickens attacks the social and economic conditions in England and satirises the whole system of laissez-faire system. The "enlightened self-interest" preached by the Benthamites is, in fact unenlightened cruelty. It is the utilitarian economists and their supporters who are responsible for poverty. They engineered the Poor Law of 1834, which set up a new system of control of poor relief. According to this Poor Law, no destitute person could get poor relief unless he entered a workhouse. The conditions in the workhouse were very miserable. All personal possessions of the poor were confiscated and there was total separation of men and women, husbands and wives.

Commenting on the Poor Law in 1836, Matthew Arnold says that "standing alone" it is bound "to embitter the feelings of the poorer classes still more." Dickens shares this view. There is, it must be added, some similarity between Elizabeth Gaskell's *Mary Barton* (1848) and Dickens's *Hard Times* (1854). Both writers denounce the soulless philosophy of Benthamite radicalism and of egoistic individualism. Although Gaskell belonged to the bourgeoisie, she still defended the interests of the working classes.

In her analysis of poverty, Gaskell never doubted that women are able to cope with poverty and are more disposed to help the poor than are men. Many male and female writers share this view. According to Charles Darwin, "woman is less selfish" and more sympathetic to the suffering of the poor than any man can ever be.

# CHAPTER 15

# COPING WITH EMOTION

I wish here to indicate how far women themselves felt self-discipline was necessary in moments of rejection, grief, jealousy, or overwhelming passion and whether such discipline came from social necessity or individual criteria regarding self-respect.

Emily in *The Prime Minister* goes through many interesting and extremely honest phases in her feelings. When Arthur Fletcher comes to say good-bye to her, she genuinely wishes he had kissed her. Yet, although not a coquette, she knows through cleverly analysed thought that she does not love him "as men and women love." Troloppe shows us her meditations after he has left. She "loved" him before and yet had taught herself in a "confused and perplexed lesson" that it wasn't real love. Now she wonders if her father's wish for her to dismiss Arthur, in those early days, had really "schooled" her (chapter 17). She has now pledged herself to Ferdinand Lopez and it is too late wonder if she has made a mistake. However, by chapter 29 she is again honest enough to admit to herself that "The god of her idolatry was but a little human creature and that she should not have worshipped at so poor a shrine." Victorian mores may have been at work when she previously "tried to quench her judgement," but timeless humanity comes through and "her intellect was too strong even for her heart." Later when she is a widow and knows she will meet Arthur again, there is refreshing truth. "When a woman really loved a man, as she loved this man, there is a desire to touch him which quivers at her fingers' ends."

Then pride steps in. "What! Should she be known to love again after such a catastrophe?" All is naturally resolved in the end, but Emily, privately, is not the mealie-mouthed endurer that one sometimes meets in nineteenth-century novels. In different circumstances one admires similar honesty on the part of Rhoda Fleming when she reads Dahlia's "honeymoon" letters. Rhoda contemplates that such passion as Dahlia expresses might tempt some women "To abandon principle and the bondage of the hereafter for such a long delicious gulp of divine life." She is ashamed after reflection of such thoughts and yet realises that "many, many passionate hearts that she could feel as her own would be ready" to behave as Dahlia (chapter 9). Meredith is probably more capable than Rhoda herself of abandoning "divine sanctions" even vicariously, but, nevertheless it is something that a male author could admit that women might feel strong passion equal to their own sex. In the case of *Jane Eyre*, one feels her all-night struggles are with self-respect as Charlotte Bronte, though a minister's daughter, may be aware from her own personal struggles that "divine sanctions" are easier to picture before and after, rather than during such crises!

The chapter headed "History of a Self-Tormentor" in *Little Dorrit* (chapter 21) indicates that Miss Wade has a violent temper, which she controls in an unusual way. She is hungry for the love of her school fellows and then as a governness for that of her pupils. Once she has found she is illegitimate, she becomes more and more bitter and more and more sensitive to "patronage" and "condescension" even when Dickens hints the occasions are imaginary. Even when a young man falls in love with her, she hates him to praise her for her looks (as if she had nothing else to offer). She practically drives him into the arms of his cousin and then, of course, resents it all. How far all this is due to Society's attitude to illegitimacy and how far to an obsessively touchy nature it is difficult to discern, much as we are bound to be influenced by her warped treatment of Tattycoram, as the Meagles call the little maid who eventually returns to them in the realisation that they do genuinely care for her. Miss Wade is only interesting here in that her self-discipline is very strong and may not lead to happiness but certainly shows a unique spiritness, misguided or otherwise.

The second Mrs. Gibson in *Wives and Daughters* appears—especially in Molly's eyes—to be very insensitive to all deep emotions. Yet, apparently, the death of her first husband was shattering, at the time, to her." For if ever Mrs. Gibson felt anything acutely it was the death of Mr. Kirkpatrick and, amiably callous as she was in most things, she recoiled from exposing her daughter wilfully to the same kind of suffering which she herself had experienced" (Gaskell: *Wives and Daughters*, chapter 35). The comment refers to Cynthia's and Mrs. Gibson's earlier plans for matchmaking with Osborne Hamley until she "overheard" her husband mention complex symptoms of the aorta to the boy's father. Among the gentry whom she so admires, she may have felt it good taste to hide the reality of her young grief, but whatever the motive of her earlier self-control, it had been exercised. Molly, on the other hand, when she first heard that her father was to marry again, shows no sense of control and her jealousy is passionate. She is later to have many occasions to be temperate for her father's sake and, in any case, is very young at this point of the book besides being an extremely devoted daughter. As John McVeagh in *Elizabeth Gaskell* (chapter 19) remarks: "This is Molly's initiation into hardship; change and separation are the law of life. She learns, after a protected childhood, pain and disappointment come unchecked and one's only defence is one's resilience." Dr. Gibson has not really told her in a very tactful manner, although leaving to the last moment was really for her benefit. In fact the whole marriage is meant to protect his unsheltered Molly. At the time she cannot see this and can feel only "bitter grief'; "suppressed passion—"; "mental suffering" (chapter 10). All the more credit to her, therefore, that she later, for her father's sake, shows tact and generosity of spirit to her new stepmother.

Facing up to reality when life takes a new turn is handled in *Middlemarch* in varying ways according to the depth of the character in the first place and the strength of the emotions involved in the differing situations. Harriet Bulstrode, for instance, is criticised for various vanities throughout the book, but when her husband's crisis comes, she strips herself of all worldly things, realises her true affection for her husband and, when she looks at him, "A movement of new compassion and old tenderness went through her—" (Eliot: *Middlemarch* chapter 74)". Dorothea, on the other hand, has no real love, old or new, to sustain her but when she wakes up to real life from her idealistic dreams, she feels a true compassion for Casaubon when she realises, through casual words of Will's that his researches have all been "done" in German fields of thought already. "A new alarm on his behalf which was the first stirring of a pitying tenderness fed by the realities of his lot and not by her own dreams" (chapter 21).

On a different plane, the ever-selfish Rosamund does come to something like awareness of her husband's worth after Dorothea's soul-searching talk with her, pointing out that Lydgate had to come to her with all his recent reverses because he felt that Rosamund could not be made to suffer in any way because of her "sensitive nature" (despite the fact that her own extravagance has contributed greatly to his downfall). But now Rosamund is "under the first shock that had shattered her dream-world in which she was easily confident of herself and critical of others." Of course, unlike Harriet and Dorothea, this "shattering" will not make her a very much pleasanter person, but still learns to be more of a wife and less of a child (chapter 81). What is interesting here, to a modern commentator, is that just as Charlotte Bronte expected Jane Eyre and Lucy Snowe to discipline themselves, no matter how strong their emotions, so also does George Eliot expect it of a strong, or gradually-learning female character. Is this because they are women themselves and know woman *can* so behave? Does the male author like the clinging little woman to display her feelings so that a hero can "comfort" her? Of course all this depends on the author's own nature.

Thackeray with his acerbic outlook obviously prefers Lady Castlewood when she gets a grip on herself, so to speak, and, having made an idol of her husband and having found out he is unfaithful, gradually realises he is also her intellectual inferior and "Her spirit rebelled and she disowned any more obedience" (*Virginias* chapter 9). Dickens on the other hand veers between childlike doting Dora and capable-if ever-angelic Agnes. Speaking through David Copperfield, nevertheless he does seem to convey that delightful, winning approaches over inability to housekeep might wear a man down in the end! When it comes to the crunch, however, Dora is self-controlled enough to master any fear of death she must have had in concern for "her boy." In the big moments of life or death, evidently a heroine, no matter how spoilt and immature, must suddenly grow up. In *Barnaby Rudge*, Dennis the hangman ponders concerning Mr. Gashford in his dealings with Emma Haredale that he had better beware as "She's one of those fine, black-eyed proud girls as I wouldn't trust at times with a knife" (chapter 59). Up to this point, Emma has behaved in a perfectly "womanly" way—although obviously showing more character and intelligence than, say, Dolly Varden. Gashford is merely hinting through his own code of thought that the obnoxious Dennis will not be able to just "help himself" as Sim Tappertit would probably have put it, had things reached that point! In short, the swooning female has only a limited use in fiction, to offset any stridency a male might fear. The hideous Miggs manages to be both strident and swooning when it suits her, in fact.

I would like to say a little in this chapter about women's sexual awareness: a "little," in that very little is overtly suggested in nineteenth-century literature, especially among the single girls—which is not to say that more consciousness was not felt in real life among the less sheltered maidens! In *The Professor*, Crimond ironically wonders why, if Mdlle Reuterse's young ladies were reared in utter unconsciousness of vice and the precautions used to protect them, if not innocent were innumerable. The net result was that having attained the age of fourteen, not one of these girls could look a man in the face with modesty (chapter 12). Charlotte Bronte insinuates through the medium of Crimond that this may be due to the girls' Roman Catholic upbringing! He argues rather tortuously, that in an over-stress on purity, the Church has made them prurient. Nice Protestants, especially English, girls are not so afflicted. Yet Ginevra Fanshawe in *Villette* seems far from innocent and she fulfills both religious and national advantages, so upbringing again, supposedly comes into it.

In *Diana of the Crossways*, the heroine is enabled to be honest about her lack of *passion* for Dacey as long as she did not receive direct questioning, which would "pierce to the bottom of the heart." But what enabled her the more easily to deceive herself? We are referred to the "fiction of a perfect ignorant innocence combined with common intelligence," which normally governs women of the times but still told that Diana had more knowledge of life than that but just wanted "to stay on the shore" of morality and cling as long as she could to her reputation (chapter 21). The poor young woman realises that women can be weak but thinks that facing up to possible temptations and making step by step precautions she can be strong (chapter 23). When Dacier proposes she is amazed by the force of her love "—despite the many hooded messengers it had despatched to her of late" (chapter 25). Easy for us to say today she wanted her cake and eat it, but her earlier marriage had been a failure. Yet, she was still, in law, bound by it and Dacier's friendship had been mentally refreshing and stimulating: what was regarded as a "stained name" at that time would affect her life as a woman more than his, wherever they escaped to.

In the *Eustace Diamonds*, Lucinda Ronaoake had submitted to the engagement with Sir Griffin, has had many raging quarrels with him, yet presses on because of her, and her aunt's poverty ("poverty" in the Society's sense). On the night before the wedding, she states vehemently to her aunt, "I know I shall never see him again. I will never trust myself alone in his presence . . . when he touches me, my whole body is in agony. To be kissed by him is madness" (chapter 69). Rather last minute one might feel, but Trollope and other Victorian writers lead us, delicately, to believe that the cold-hearted proceed with rich marriages despite sexual antipathy and the sexually ignorant wake up, alas, too late. Obviously Lucinda was knowledgeable and reasonably ruthless but not when she finally faced up to herself (and the nature of Sir Griffin!)

In a different world, Rosa Budd in *Edwin Drood* is very young and overprotected, but she is aware that Jasper is wooing without words, when he watches her so closely while he is playing the piano at the Crisparkle's dinner-party. She tells Helena later, "As I was singing I felt terrified but besides that ashamed and passionately hurt. It was as if he had kissed me and I couldn't bear and cried out" (chapter 7). Almost a child in her normal reactions, Rosa is obviously woman enough to sense physical effrontery and to deal with it in her own way.

In *The Return of the Native*, Hardy tells us that Wildeve had those looks that "No man would have seen anything to admire and no woman anything to dislike" (chapter 5). As Wildeve is what is generally referred to as a philosopher, this does not say much for women's self-analysis of their feelings of physical attraction! In fact, a few sentences before, Hardy has referred to Wildeve's whole body being that of a "pantomimie expression of a lady-killing carrier." But what does this amount to? Many of Hardy's heroes are completely bewitched by beautiful but completely worthless young ladies—and such young men have not been particularly "sheltered." As has been mentioned before, married ladies seem to be more able "to get away with" sexual references than a single girl and, in the case of Lady Carbury, we have a (dubious) "Society" lady and a writer. She is thus enabled to say to an editor, regarding her Criminal Queens series, "Of all these royal and luxurious sinners, it was their chief sin that—they consented to be playthings rather than wives. I have striven hard to be proper, but when girls read everything why should not an old woman write everything?" Of course there is a double hypocrisy here in that Lady Carbury would be most effronted if any of her male admirers in the literary set *really* thought of her as old together with the fact that only a young girl of a "fast" nature would be seen reading "anything."

Thackeray's Blanche Amory admitted to reading French romances, but no doubt she read them in secret. On the other hand, dubious actions mistakenly undertaken by otherwise much-respected women should not be judged too hastily. This point is stressed by those writing later in the century, as one would expect of course. There is also a difference between Meredith's Diana doing extra ordinarily foolish things (by her contemporaries' standards) and expecting all to judge her by her best friend's standards and the furious resentment of Hardy's Thomasine to village gossip when circumstances alone have led her into mishap. Although women were never allowed to be accompanied by men on a long journey, obviously a woman's own normal morals should be taken into account. "Anyone who knows how pure she is would feel any such thought to be unjust"—that is, the thought that Tamsie should have slept with Wildeve on the unfortunate night away from home, brought about by his mismanagement of the wedding registration (Hardy: *Return of the Native*, Book 1, chapter 11). Thomasine takes up the point later with self-respect showing through her firm manner! "I am to be a warning to others—why don't people judge me by my acts—do I look like a lost woman?" (*Ibid* chapter 2, Book 2). This may all sound rather priggish, but one forgets that men on the whole set the standards by insisting on a virgin bride: even if the virginity had only been marred by a cloud on a woman's "name."

Similarly with Eustacia Vye, she bitterly remarks that because she has "a bad name she is obliged to act by stealth, not because I do ill, but because others are pleased to say so" (*Return of the Naive* chapter 5, Book 4). Mind you, Eustacia acts considerably more foolishly than Thomasine would ever dream of. My point is that village gossip of the time built up an atmosphere in which a woman took the whole blame for even mere foolishness. . . .! Wildeve, in his own way, is just as self-dramatising and indiscreet as Eustacia but gets away with it for a long time.

In a different world, Disraeli shows us the struggles of a famous actress—"Though not stainless in conduct, she was pure in spirit." Then again, "She required that devotion which she had yielded, and she had separated herself from the being for whom she had made the most precious sacrifice. He offered her the consoling compensation of a settlement which she refused." In other words, Stella had high standards for a profession not famed for morality, and had only "yielded" to someone whom she adored, had a child by him only to discover that he was a roué with little devotion for anyone. (*Coningsby* chapter 6, Book 4). When Stella dies, Disraeli tells his readers, "she had exercised many virtues which elsewhere may perhaps be accepted as some palliation of one great error." Admittedly her great successes as an actress evidently puts her on a different plane in some Victorian eyes from the Eustacias of this world, but at least Stella really loved and despised being "paid off." Eustacia, on the other hand, loves Wildeve—at least sometimes—only when he is ignoring her: playing at his love.

All in all, coping with emotion was a very tricky business for Victorian literary characters, whatever happened in real life. When literature is obviously being used as a vehicle for setting up a "model" for real-life women, the female author veered towards self-control as the guiding star whereas men vary between charming displays of so-called womenly weakness and a general "pull-yourself-together" attitude when the said women might be an embarrassment to male characters. On the other hand, peeps at real life by both male and female writers indicate that genuine feelings were as difficult to control as one would expect today and synthetic feelings equally detectable.

# CHAPTER 16

# READY WIT AND OUTSPOKENNESS AMONG WOMEN

As critics have often observed, it is in conversation that characters either show themselves completely or through their "woodenness" lose our interest completely. In the same way, the emerging strength and independence of Victorian women is often seen in sharp, quick thoughtful sayings, which indicate much humour and intelligence behind the scenes of the most well-conducted woman. If any kicking against the goad of their narrow lot was going on, it seemed to burst out in such repartee. Sometimes the author in question does not surprise us as she or he has led up to such personality developments. In other cases, it is as if unwittingly the author lets out some snippet he or she has heard in real life, even if it is at variance with perfect propriety!

When Paul, through shyness, asks Phyllis what is in her basket, she retorts, "potatoes!" though it is perfectly plain that it is a basket of eggs. He angrily demands why she made such a reply. To which her answer is "What *do you* mean by asking what they were when it is perfectly plain to be seen?" (*Cousin Phyllis*, chapter 1, Part 1). Hard on Paul, in a sense, but refreshing that the girl should be irritated by small-talk. Similarly, Ethel Newcome is criticised by Thackeray for being "Too impatient of dullness and pomposity." Fair enough, but we should be glad to read that this is related to an intolerance of "affection or insincerity" in others (*Pendennis*, Part 1, chapter 24). Her creator may feel that suffering in later life will do Ethel good in that it will soften the sarcasm in her, but at least Lord Farintosh admires her because she is "The cleverest and wittiest girl in England" (chapter 59). When Pendennis himself says to Laura, "I hate clever women" (chapter 23), she says, "Thank you" in the same dry manner as an intelligent woman of today. The matter is not helped by the fact that we have recently heard that Blanche Amory "writes poems—composes music." Supposedly this is charming or artistic rather than "clever" or perhaps it depends on whom Pen is infatuated with at the time of speaking! Depending on the hero, wit is considered charming or a sign of a sharp character to be avoided. Of course the heroines would only moderate their speech if father or admirer had indicated too often that it had signs of a shrew.

When the mischievous Hetty sees that Harry Warrington confuses Persia with Prussia, she "allowed her tongue to wag in a more than usual saucy way—she made a hundred sly allusions to their guest. She introduced Prussia and Persia into their conversations with abominable pertness and frequency" (chapter 23, Part 1, *Virginians*. Now, we know that Hetty does everything with great charm and is childish in nature compared to Theo, so, of course, "abominable" is used by Thackeray with a tender humour. He always admits that his creation is intelligent, but the barbed wit is only permissible because she is somewhat "kittenish"—though not in an irritating, self-conscious way.

Far more fierce and deliberate is the bitter sarcasm of Ethel Newcome. Groomed by her grandmother for the marriage-market, she still resents it underneath and in chapter 38 of *The Newcomes*, she flashes out, "Do you suppose it is nothing to me to be bandied about from bidder to bidder and offered for sale to a gentleman who will not have me?" Significantly, this is the last chapter in Part 1 and we may be meant to deduce that Ethel's "better self" will now begin to surface through the luxuries and power over men she has become used to. In the previous chapter, she has already remarked savagely to her grandmother, "We are as much sold as Turkish women; the only difference being that our masters may have but one Circassian at a time—No, there is no freedom for us." The old lady is an intimidating person, but having spoilt Ethel, she cannot be surprised that the lively girl rounds on her.

In a different world, Frances rounds on Hunsden, fearless of his crushing remarks, although she is, seemingly, a timid person. "Your method is to squeeze the sap out of the creation and make manure of the refuse, by turning it to what you call use" (*The Professor* chapter 24). Her life has been too hard and her nature too essentially serious for this to be wit, but as the conversation progresses, she shows she is a match for the forceful Hunsden, who, partly to tease her, belittles Switzerland as a merchandising, servile country in a spirit of debate, little expecting a woman, even one loved by Crimsworth whom he knows to be highly discriminating, to answer him with such force.

Woman who are not attractive or young have a harder time getting away with either wit or outspokenness. Money, of course, helps. Miss Dunstable of Framley Court is lively and frank, fearing neither God nor man, but she is not necessarily admired by Troloppe or his readers of that time. In chapter 8 of *Framley Parsonage*, she suggests that her poodle had better not be kept with the duke's dogs . . . "how his morals would be destroyed!" The duke pertinently asks if the remark is meant to be personal, but she "turns away to the fire," and he and we are left to draw our own conclusions. When Miss Dunstable much later marries the doctor, one feels that she is doing the most sensible thing of her life in Trollope's eyes—though she makes it clear her tongue will be as free as ever.

Mrs. Cadwallader in *Middlemarch* often "gets away with murder" in her speech, but is this partly because she is from the upper class and kind at heart? In chapter 38 she refers scathingly to Casaubon as "Thomas Aquinas" and Ladislaw as a "sort of Byronic hero,": suggesting that this is how they see themselves. For some figures in Parliament, she also has scant respect. "They say the last unsuccessful candidate at Middlemarch—failed because he did not bribe enough" and has already described standing for Parliament as "the most expensive hobby in the world." As all this is said to Mr. Brooke, she obviously wants to tease him, but there is no question of either he or Sir James Chettam putting her down in any way (chapter 38). Shirley in the novel of that name is, of course, another person who can "get away with almost anything"—again partly because of her class but mainly because of a winning combination of strong character and charm. For instance, her views on her uncle, Mr. Sympson's mind, are trenchant. "His ideas are not clean—if he could add to his imagination the contents of Mrs. Gill's bucking-basket and let her boil it in her copper, it would do him incalculable good" (chapter 36).

Sometimes a woman character may give views that we know to be unfair yet can still admire. For Mrs. Dixon in *North and South* says of her master, "Master was born, I suppose to marry missus—but he should have loved her properly and not always been reading, reading, thinking, thinking" (Gaskell: *North & South*, chapter 16). Mr. Hale is, of course, to be heartbroken when his wife dies, but such frank thinking is still refreshing in the despised servant class. Likewise in *North and South*, Margaret can be lively and outspoken but limited, of course, by what was expected of her. When her godfather, Mr. Bell, comes to visit them, her father teasingly tells him that Margaret has become a "red" republican during her sojourn in the North. Margaret answers roundly, "It is all because I'm standing up for progress. Mr. Bell would have had it standing still at exchanging wild-beasts skins for acorns" (Chapter 40). She has not been throughout the book particularly sharp with Mrs. Thornton, but a great deal of quiet observation has obviously been going on, for when Thornton proposes, she asks him not to drive her by his sarcasm about her aunt to reproduce his mother's tone. On hearing of their engagement, she will, no doubt, say "That woman!"

Molly in *Wives and Daughters* is set in a different mould from Margaret—more impetuous, perhaps not so quietly thoughtful (though this is to grow in her). Her thoughts on her stepmother have to be suppressed for a long time to spare her father, but one day it all becomes too much for her especially regarding the latter's matchmaking which has an unscrupulous base to it, well beyond that expected of the Victorian mother. "Thank you, Miss Goodenough, when I want to be married, I'll not trouble Mamma. I'll look out for myself" (chapter 58).

Molly is easily irritated by her stepmother and it is perhaps a little unfair to pick on Miss G. who has been very good to her in the past. She feels that all the village are gossiping about her and "enough is enough." Cynthia is obviously a much more outspoken character, by nature, but her own desires to rise in the world sometimes militate against the tendency. She has her own fondness for Molly, if tempered by hidden plans of her own, and when the new Mrs. Gibson rates Molly for tomboyish ways in front of Miss Browning, Cynthia remarks sarcastically: "Please do not let us go to Miss Browning this evening. I shall pledge myself for Molly that she shan't sit in a cherry-tree; and Molly shall see that I don't go upstairs in an unladylike manner" (chapter 21).

The latter part of the remark must be particularly galling to her stepmother since the latter prided herself on the refinement of Cynthia's education. The second Mrs. Gibson acts as an irritant on young Molly likewise although the girl has told herself she must struggle to be friendly for her father's sake. Her stepmother asks her to help her with her unpacking and sit with her, petulantly remarking that Dr. Gibson could have put off his visiting for one evening. Molly is driven to exclaim, "Mr. Craven-Smith couldn't put off his dying" (chapter 15).

A woman used to running her own house is on the whole given a certain leeway. I am not referring to shrewishness, which has been

commented on in another chapter, but to a certain tone of forthrightness. In the case of Trollope, this is seen as more acceptable if mingled
with our old friend "charm." In *The Three Clerks*, Mrs. Woodward does
not suffer fools gladly. "She was slightly given to repartee" and though
averse to a fool, she could sympathise with folly" (chapter 3). This leads
her to make mistakes in estimating her daughter's suitors, but she still
looked to no man for guidance merely because he was a man. Trollope
shows us a less vivacious widow in *Rachel Raye*, but one could speak
out when her dominating elder daughter went too far. In chapter 12,
Rachel herself is driven to sarcasm when her sister calls and remarks on
Luke Rowan having just left "And you'll be likely to see him again if
you stay here, Dolly." She has said more than she meant but at least it
leads her mother to remark "And if Rachel was to like him, I don't see
why she shouldn't like somebody some day as well as other girls." Helen
Graham in *Tenant of Wildfell Hall* is used to fending for herself and
the Victorian reader, soon to be let into the secret of her apparent "single
parenthood," will not object to the fact that, fortified by the strength
of innocence, she faces the pastor fiercely. "With a kind of shameless
calmness—she as good as told me my pastoral advice was quite thrown
away upon her" (chapter 11). The vicar has taken it upon himself to
hint to Helen that rumours are circulating about her and Markham in
the village, and she more or less orders him out of the house. Helen
shows similar strong character when she warns young Esther Hargrave
that "You may as well sell yourself to slavery at once as marry a man
you dislike. If your mother and brother are unkind to you, you may
leave them, but remember you are bound to your husband for life"
(chapter 41). As I stated above, such remarks are naturally accepted as
less "bold" from one who has been through the perils of matrimony,
than from a single girl.

Many Victorian heroines are describes as having strong characters
or witty tongues without this being put on paper. I merely seek to show
that they could evidently get away with more than we imagine to have
been the case. An author may feel that direct speech is not his forte or
that inner wit, indicated indirectly, is enough—but it helps us to understand a girl like Esther in *Felix Holt* if we read of her saying "I notice
all the portraits are in a conscious, affected attitude. That fair lady Betty
looks as if she has been drilled into that position and has not even will
of her own to move again unless she had a little push given her" (chapter
40, regarding the Transome ancestors). Similarly, when Felix irritates

her earlier in the book, dismissing all fine ladies, indicating thus that true Puritans would never have married "fine-lady wives," she retorts sharply: "Oh, there is no such danger of such mésalliances. Men who are unpleasant companions and make frights of themselves are sure to get wives tasteless enough to suit them" (chapter 5). True, Esther is seen in the second quotation as still a girl, untouched by suffering—whereas in the first, she has already been described as brooding in the library, unable to read, as she is now studying the "Book of life." Perhaps she has no desire to become a Lady Betty herself, because it is not long after that she refuses Harold Transome's proposal. Yet both remarks tell us more about the inner Esther than any long descriptions would do, i.e., a girl of spirit.

Wit, a ready tongue, outspokenness may denote independence emerging in the nineteenth-century girl or, alas, it may be just one facet of the "marriageability" of a young lady for a lively, intelligent young man who may expect her, still, to buckle under in the married state. Either way, such indications do show that the strong-minded young woman who was to emerge in some circles at the end of the century, ready for a career, did not just burst forth from the head of Zeus like the legendary Minerva!

# CHAPTER 17

# WOMAN'S ATTITUDE TO PHILOSOPHY AND RELIGION

Naturally women's attitude to these subjects vary with their background and education, but it is also interesting to note in those days that we think of "conventionally religious"—how much temperament altered attitudes, be it that of the author or of the character herself.

In *Mary Barton*, Mrs. Gaskell gives a paragraph of reproach to those who comfort mourners by the phrase "it cannot be helped." She points out sternly that if a trouble "could be helped, softened, obviated, one wouldn't be mourning." Mary Barton's activity, she correctly says, gives hope to her—albeit the sad hope that she could somehow mitigate her father's guilt, of which she is not yet totally convinced, by hiding evidence that may only be tell-tale to her. She feels, as she knows, he is incapable of cold-blooded murder (chapter 22). Now she has at least some inner proof that Jem is innocent and when she speaks fiercely to Margaret on the subject, the latter points out that she herself has money put by that would pay a lawyer. She brooks no refusal from Mary, saying wisely, "There's two sides to the commandment and that we may say "Let others do unto you, as you would do unto them," for pride often prevents us giving others a great deal of pleasure, in not letting them be kind, when their hearts are longing to be kind" (chapter 23). Mrs. Gaskell herself was going through a bereft period in her own life in that her own young son, William, died, only three years before *Mary Barton* was published and the book was no doubt fermenting in her imagination long before that date. Thus when she says "It is woes that cannot in any earthly way be escaped that admit least earthly comforting" (chapter 22), it is the mother, not the minister's wife, who speaks. In *Sylvia's Lovers*, Philip quotes the words "forgive us our trespasses," but Sylvia cries passionately: "It's well enough for them as has but little to forgive to use those words" and "Him as has done harm to me and mine." I may keep from striking or murdering, but I'll never forgive." She is speaking of Simpson's evidence, which contributes to hanging her father, though later she forgives him in her heart (chapter 29). This is thoughtout, or at least, felt-out Christianity. When one turns to George Eliot, one can naturally expect something deeper because of her own philosophical studies—of course, tempered by the nature of the female character under discussion. Dorothea in *Middlemarch* has an almost Shelley-like belief that "one can widen the skirts of light making the struggle with darkness narrower—it is my belief. I have found it out and cannot part with it. I have been finding out my religion since I was a little girl. I used to pray—now I hardly ever pray. I try not to have desires for myself, because they may not be good for others, and I have too much already" (chapter 39). This could sound sanctimonious, out of context, but not if one comes to know Dorothea well. She has just as high a standard for others. Mr. Tyke, who preaches at the hospital, is not felt by her to be as admirable a Christian as a man who would 'Take in the most good of all kinds and bring in the most people as sharers of it.' Will and she have been speaking of Mrs. Tyke's recently published sermons, mainly concerning the Apocalypse, which, she feels, is of little practical use of Lowick, compared to Mr. Farebrother's kindly visits (chapter 50).

We turn now to a rather fatalistic view of religion. Disraeli's *Sybil* is passionately concerned with freedom for the working man and yet she actually believes it is wrong to fight for that cause as "I will believe that moral power is irresistible or where are we to look?" And, again, "Only those who can help themselves God helps" (chapter 5, Book 5). And this despite the fact that her father, Gerard, has been explaining to her that the people of England almost seem to need a new Battle of Hastings but with different aims. (Nor is this a violent man). In complete contrast, Margaret in *North and South*, faced with her father's "schismatic" future, gazes into the universe "seeing at every moment some farther distance, and yet no sign of God!" (chapter 5). She changes this mood when her father later asks her to join him in the Lord's Prayer, but at least her long period of introspection proves she can think things out for herself. Later, she is to use the "Nuremburg" story to illustrate to Mr. Thornton that, just as the man in the story brought up his son so sheltered from the world he was unable to cope with real life when that father died, so the workers could not be "benevolently" protected by Mr. Thornton even in their leisure hours, if they were ever going to be truly emancipated. Her philosophy of life is much deeper than his in this long discussion—even though he obviously feels that it is based on total ignorance of industrial life.

She keeps the conversation on a human level, but at one point says strongly: "God has made us so we must be mutually dependent—neither you or any master can help yourselves. The most proudly independent man depends on those around him for insensible influence on his character—his life" (chapter 15). In *Mary Barton,* the invalid Margaret can be acerbic in general relationships, but her religion teaches her patience, saying that it is demanded by God. "Ay, my dear, being patient is the hardest work we, any of us, have to do through life. Waiting is far more difficult than doing. I've known that about my sight, and many have known it through watching the sick; but it's one of God's lessons we all must learn, one way or another (chapter 12). Easy to say this is too simple or it is merely Mrs. Gaskell's view of life as a minister's wife. But if one studies Margaret's sharp tongue and frank outlook in other fields, one realises it is part and parcel of her—no mere convention. Like Sybil (above) it may be a little "fatalistic," but there is little Mary can do but wait, whereas Sybil, not being a peace-lover by nature, knows well that a class struggle—with emphasis on the struggle—is the only way to change.

Some Victorian women in novels "question" not so much "the words of the Bible as others use them."* When Philip in *Sylvia's Lovers* uses "Forgive us our trespasses as we forgive"—Sylvia cannot but disagree, stressing that it is easy for some to use these words. Religious feelings are more complex and she just can "never forgive" those who have done any wrong to her or have denigrated her (chapter 29 regarding Simpson's evidence towards hanging her father). On the other side of the coin, Esther in *Mary Barton* cannot even imagine that those who love her could "Love her in the next world!" She incorporates this is an account to Jem of nightly visions of her dead Mother and baby sister, trailing round her bed with sad stoney eyes—they don't turn back either but pass behind the head of the bed and I feel their eyes on me everywhere" (chapter 14). This speaks much for a stern upbringing and little true knowledge of the Gospel. Jem is moved by her feelings and wishes he could do something for her, but seems to have no words to imply

---

*This is Northern dialect! (Yorkshire)—still spoken.

the dead might have similar compassion. Job, in the same book, practically boasts that he does not pray regularly, except for having the odd word with the Almighty. He says that Mary should avoid the company of Sally, who may be "—good-natured—jolly—full of fun" but is for reasons such as these more likely to lead one astray. "Do you think folk could be led astray by one who was every way bad?" (chapter 25). Evidently a woman must give example of life and prayer, but a man may be content with preaching. This is not to deny that Job is a virtuous and admirable man but merely to state that religion may seem more "embarrassing" than general ethics to him. Although his grand-daughter may be more explicit though with her blindness it is, naturally, one would expect, more difficult to pray or to speak of patience. Mind you, Margaret, if called upon would have been as condemning of Sally had she been present. Similarly, in Trollope's *Framley Parsonage*, although Mark is the parson, it is Fanny who cries out against his curses when the bailiffs move in. "Do not wish him evil, Mark; you may be sure he has troubles of his own" and "Vengeance is mine, saith the Lord, leave that to Him; and for us all let us pray that he may soften the hearts of all" (chapter 44). Yet it is Mark who has involved Sowerby in Fanny's life by his own gambling, and Fanny who, until now has been unaware of this habit, will suffer more. Nor is she a "goody-goody" heroine and she can be jealous, uncharitable, and irritable among friends and family.

When one turns to Thomas Hardy, of course, one does not expect the thinking characters to be committed to conventional religion. Before Tess meets Angel, she is singing to herself a paen to God, while her soul is closer to a form of Pantheism. In *Jude the Obscure*, Sue has a "religious position" in that she carves pious statuary, but she is far more attracted by pagan statues, buying an Apollo and Cupid from a foreign pedlar, though at that time feeling a little guilty about it, (part 2, chapter 3). But this of course is only the beginning of her doubts regarding the accepted beliefs. Once she meets Jude, she is not merely influenced by him but reveals to him many thoughts of a pagan nature long harboured by her, though she has not had a suitable companion with whom to share them. However after the deaths of her children, and the birth of a stillborn child so soon after, she cries to Jude, "We must conform! All the ancient wrath of the Power above us has been vented upon us—and it is no good fighting against God." Jude stringently points out that they have been fighting " . . . against man and senseless circumstance" (Part 6, chapter 3). At this she admits that she is becoming "As superstitious as a senseless savage," but this alters little for her as she still feels "cowed into submission" (Ibid.) She becomes more and more glossy and begins to think that she suffered so much because of her lack of humility in life, hitherto. Jude is amazed and cries out, "You have been a fearless feeler, both as a thinker and a feeler, and you deserved more admiration than I gave. I was too full of narrow dogmas at that time to see it. Alas, for it is emotionally based and not rationally." She takes to haunting the little local church, haunted by the idea that it is because she broke her "sacramental vows to Phillotson." She has been punished by the unnatural deaths of her children. Jude pities her deeply, but he is driven to say "Is a woman a thinking unit at all or only a fraction wanting its integer? How you argued that marriage was only a clumsy contract—if two and two made four when we were happy together, surely they make four now?" (Ibid.). To be fair to poor Sue, it is the unselfish thought of Arabella's child, also hunged, which has sent her over the edge, since Arabella has recently visited them—but then Sue could not see, as Jude did, that Arabella has recently visited them—but then Sue could not see, as Jude did, that Arabella's grieving was very superficial, as she had cared little for the younger Jude when he was alive. When Sue finally not only returns to Phillotson, but after one passionate meeting with Jude suggests that they break the habit of not sleeping together—as an exculpation for her renewed love for Jude, it is too much for the latter. Jude, hearing of the news from Mrs. Edlin, cries out: "Our ideas were fifty years too soon to be any good to us. And so the resistance they met brought reaction in her and—ruin on me" (Part 6, chapter 10).

Superficial religious observances had by this era often become social habits, which could be referred back to religion, if a person was questioned too deeply about this problem. Dickens, we know, points out in *Great Expectations* how cruel it is to inflict on Joe Gargery all the "trapping" of a funeral—weeping bands around one's hat, special gloves, and the inevitable artificial mourners and pay tear-shedders. But, women, it seems, often take these things as almost conforming until we come to Mary Barton who says very bluntly "This will cost a pretty penny. I often wonder why folk wear mourning—it costs a great deal of money when folk can spare it least, and, if what the Bible tells us is true, we ought not to be sorry when a friend, who has been good· has gone to his rest; and as for a bad man, one's glad enough to get shut on him" (E. Gaskell: *Mary Barton*, chapter 5). This may even seem hard, but she is helping Margaret out with the making of very expensive dresses for a poor woman whose husband beat her whenever he was drunk and who has left her very little money.

From a different standpoint, Mrs. Gaskell is ashamed of Sylvia going to a funeral "just for the sensation of it" and finds it typical of "the modern girl" that she should leave her parents to cope in order to do so. On the other hand, Sylvia herself can admire Hester for sitting with the bedridden sister of the dead man, crying out "How good she is" (*Sylvia's Lovers*, chapter 7). Thus quite clearly, to Sylvia, a funeral is a kind of outing whereas the real Christianity lies in the ministering to the living (even if it doesn't cross her mind to emulate Hester!).

Religion and a general philosophical outlook on life seem to the heroines I have mentioned to be governed either by the amount of suffering the women encounter in their lives, by paternal example, or by a thoughtful questioning into themselves. Hypocrisy and shallowness are left to the worldly and sceptical: the Lizzie Eustaces or the Rosa Dartles.

The nineteenth century continued to live on the traditions and thoughts that it inherited from the piety of previous generations and it was only by slow degrees that it became aware that its religious foundations were quickly eroded by nonreligious elements. The writer who described in the *Dublin Review* in 1846 the Victorian age as the age of religion expressed in "religious novels" was too optimistic and even ignorant of the religious and anti-religious movements that existed in utilitarian male-dominated society.

Some modernists tended to deify the evolutionary process, making it the source of progress. Darwin denied that he had ever been atheistic in thought, although he admitted that he had been agnostic. According to him, evolution is not incompatible with Christian religion. Darwin met George Eliot and, although their relations were friendly, Eliot unflinchingly rejected both Darwin's "evolutionism" and his "agnosticism." She thought that Darwin's presentation of biological and religious phenomena were far from "being impressive."

Although George Eliot refused to accept "any set of doctrines as a creed" in her earlier period of life, in her later philosophy of life she became convinced that Christianity is the most perfect religion. "I see in it," she writes in *Scenes of Clerical Life*, "the brightest expression of the religious sentiment that has yet found its place in the history of mankind." In her view, Christianity is simple, tolerant, and pragmatic.

Unlike Jane Austen, who did not like Evangelicalism, George Eliot was a devout supporter of the Evangelical movement. In England, the Evangelical movement came as a reaction to the deists. Deists stood for a rationalising rather than for a spiritual impulse and for "natural religion" in opposition to revealed religion. They attacked the institutional church and traditional Christianity. Most people in England were hostile to deistic beliefs. Thomas Carlyle spoke scornfully of "an absentee God, sitting idle ever since the first Sabbath at the outside of His universe."

Deism was short-lived, lasting from the end of the seventeenth to the end of the eighteenth century. Deism in England was preceded by Puritanism, which remained an influential force throughout the nineteenth century. Herbert Spencer became a lapsed Puritan and rejected all forms of religion.

While asserting an "Absolute Reality" behind appearances in the mundane world, Spencer held that this reality "transcends both human knowledge and perception." In his works, including *The Man versus the State*, he rejects the revelation and the theories of Christians. While admitting in *The Principles of Sociology* that there are "good and false" elements in religion and science, Spencer stresses that "one truth must grow ever clearer—the truth that there is an Inscrutable Existence everywhere manifested to which one can neither find nor conceive either beginning or end."

Spencer was a philosophical agnostic. Bentham was a tacit atheist. What they have in common is that they substituted self-interest in place of God. For Spencer, God is, what T. H. Huxley calls, "the Absolute *redivivus*" or a sort of "the ghostly Unknowable". Huxley adds that he "prefers the good old name God." Bentham simplified his conception of God by declaring that "God is a fictitious entity." He makes no distinction between revealed and natural religion and dismisses both as harmful to the principle of utility.

In *Past and Present*, Thomas Carlyle accuses the Victorian age of worshiping "mammonism" and the so-called "greatest happiness principle." In fact, he stresses, the age is characterised by godlessness and irreligion. "Man has lost his soul and vainly seeks antiseptic salt," falsely believing he will save it. Carlyle was the implacable foe of the utilitarian radicalism of Bentham and of Spencerian agnosticism because they were more interested in promoting possessive individualism than the salvation of souls.

It was not the supposed conflict of science and religion in the nineteenth-century that prompted intellectual doubt about the veracity of religious beliefs. It was rather the emergence of various sectarian movements in Christianity, each claiming to be a return to original Christianity, that led either to the questioning of Christian doctrines or to agnosticism.

Luther and Calvin defended individualism and the principle of inequality. They individualised piety. Calvinism, which became the doctrine of English Puritans, cast a gloom over the whole of human life. All human activities, including literature, were discouraged as being tainted by the wickedness of man's fallen nature. Like utilitarianism, Puritanism glorified the economic virtues and helped to create the business man.

The main weakness of Protestantism has always been its tendency to division and subdivision. It is this tendency that has perplexed the attitudes of men and women towards Christian religion. Jane Austen disliked all forms of "noisy religion" and remained a steady supporter of Anglican Christianity. Like Jane Austen, Charlotte Bronte is critical of "religious righteousness" or "noisy religion," which "should not be confounded" with true religion.

Most Victorian writers, including Jane Austen, Elizabeth Gaskell, George Eliot, Matthew Arnold, and Thomas Green, have rejected fatalistic and pantheistic interpretation of religion. English Puritans allowed Christian believers to forget that God is essentially love rather than power. This attitude inevitably led to fatalism, which Elizabeth Gaskell strongly rejects in her novel *Mary Barton*. Thomas Hardy's characters in his writings reflect a mixture of fatalism and pantheism.

Fatalism is the superstitious acceptance of unnecessary evil based, as Elizabeth Gaskell indicates, on a false belief in human impotence to do anything about it. As a temper, it is the tendency to false beliefs in order to excuse inaction. Christianity rejects both fatalism and pantheism. Pantheism personalises the All and worships an impersonal principle, which is incompatible with the Christian belief in God who is the complete and perfect Personality.

In the Victorian age, fatalism and determinism have been challenged by theologians, philosophers, and literary figures as counsels of despair. In our age, they are challenged for the first time in history by men of science. The challenge has come through the study of the atom by the new methods of quantum mechanics.

Since the time immemorial, men and women have believed that there is something absolute and eternal in human nature. All known races have a religion, and social anthropologists generally agree that religion is a universal phenomenon. Karl Marx, however, preached atheism and argued, unlike any writer in nineteenth-century England, that "man makes religion." Ignoring psychology altogether, he rejects all abstract theodicies, including the Christian "cult of the abstract man." In *Capital* he indicates that this cult is most prominent in Protestantism, deism, and Puritanism, which are "the most suitable religions for the bourgeoisie." Marx has failed to prove that "man creates religion."

Religion is a part of human nature and man cannot create religion just as he cannot create hunger. The whole movement of the human spirit is unintelligible without God who is the object of our worship and the final ground of our faith and hope.

# CHAPTER 18

# SOME THOUGHTS ON "WOMEN'S WEAPONS"

Among some modern males and some more dominating women, it has sometimes been the habit to speak of tears, cajolement, or general winsomeness as the "weapons" of weaker woman. If that is the case in the days of woman's liberation, what must it have been like when, in theory, it was all they had? As one might expect, the more forceful women writers had as little time for this as their sisters today.

George Eliot, naturally, had much that was caustic to say about insipidity and flirtatious exaggeration. In *Middlemarch,* one reads of "The white soft living substance—that makes its way in spite of opposing rock," referring to Rosamund's ability to "manage her papa" (chapter 36) and, later, when she is married to Lydgate, he is to discover that all her cleverness, which he once had thought was "the receptive kind which became a woman," was in fact "of the close network that was aloof and independent" (chapter 58). This is after the miscarriage brought on by her stubbornness in riding, but even in after times when life has given her a certain chastening, she "remains inflexible in judgement" and was "able to frustrate him by strategem" (Finale). Hetty in *Adam Bede* is a flirt by instinct and some harsh things are said by her more mannish creator, and yet much that she does is only "natural" . . . ladies, so-called, in works by other authors are more consciously practising an art.

In *The Way We Live Now,* Mrs. Hurtle flirts with Paul in a special way in that she is re-enacting her behaviour in America in order to revive his love. "Much of this curl-tossing, hand-patting—comes of nature but sometimes by art—of such art as there may be in it. Mrs. Hurtle was a perfect master." Paul, of course, was naive and would not observe the "art," but evidently more sophisticated men were not always flattered by it. In "A Laodician," Paula pales so dramatically when Somerset is seemingly run over by a train. He actually wonders whether her disposition is so oblique and insincere that she is "trifling, coquetting or any way making a fool of him" (chapter 12).

Admittedly, Somerset is very modest and very conscious that Paula is very rich and intellectually gifted. Nevertheless, coquetry must have taken extraordinary forms in Victorian times for him to even have these thoughts! Later, when he knows Paula better, he reflects bitterly. "History has revealed that a supernumerary lover or two is rarely considered a disadvantage by a woman, from queen to cottage-girl" (chapter 13). Paula, of course, is more complex than this, but, by contrast, little Rosa Budd, in *Edwin Drood* is "kittenish," "playful," "impish" towards Edwin mainly through a sort of irritation when they are forced to be engaged by the conditions of the will. The far more forceful Helena remarks to Rosa "There is a fascination in you," to which Rosa replies (half in jest, half in earnest!): "What a pity Master Eddy doesn't feel it more" (chapter 6).

Even Sue in *Jude the Obscure*, for all her independence of mind, admitted that she started with flirtation "The craving to attract and captivate" going further to say " . . . it began with the selfish craving to make your heart ache for me without letting mine ache for you" (chapter 3, part 6). A jilt, of course, was worse than a flirt and although Mary Barton is suspected at first by Jem as being a flirt (regarding Harry Carson), he eventually decides "She is a good girl at heart, though may be a bit set up with her beauty" (chapter 15). Both the sewing girls and old Job indicate in their own ways what would be thought if she "jilted" Jem. Job tells her that as far as regarding Jem as guilty of murdering Harry "I'm loath enough to do it, lass, but I think he has been ill-used and jilted, that's plain truth, Mary, hard as it may seem—and his blood has been up—many a man has done it from like causes" (chapter 22). One must remember that in society men rather enjoyed the flattery of being flirted with unless it overstepped certain bounds. She must, in fact, appear not to be infringing some code set by her fellow-women. As Meredith says in *Rhoda Fleming*, "Men's faith in women is uneasy, unstable and changeable however deeply they may be charmed" (chapter 21).

Nancy Pratt in *Sylvia's Lovers* praises Sylvia to Philip because, unlike many other girls, "she is no flirt." Most flirting girls are always "gape-gazing to catch other folk's eyes in order to see what is thought of them" (chapter 12).

Conscious flirtation was obviously a "weapon" in that the marriage-market was almost a girl's only profession. Let us return for a moment to Mary Barton. Although Margaret found it very difficult to comprehend the temptations of Mary, her creator Mrs. Gaskell explains thoughtfully "She (Margaret) had no idea of the strength of conflict between will and principle in some who were differently constituted from herself." She has already explained to the reader that "loveliness, vanity, ambition, or the desire of being admired exposes so many" (chapter 22). Here then Mary is not thinking of a rich marriage but acting on a basic instinct to win admiration.

Disraeli in *Coningsby* speaks of a more pleasing side to coquetry: "A being who wishes to please . . . t'is a career that requires great abilities, infinite pains, a gay and airy spirit" (book 3, chapter 2). What a waste all this charm seems, if it is merely to soothe the savage breast—but the idea evidently is that this sort of thing kept the wheels of society going!

In *Diana of the Crossways*, Miss Paynham is wrong about Diana, but her views are interesting, nevertheless. "Deductively, the lady who inspired the passion in numbers of gentlemen and set herself to win their admiration with her lively display of dialogue must be coquettish; she could hold them only by her coldness. Anecdotes, epigrams, drolleries do not bubble to the lips of a woman who is under an emotional spell" (chapter 28). Meredith has earlier explained that Miss Paynham, though prim, is "pursued by ideas of sex in analysing the direct motive of every person around her." Diana, as we know, genuinely believes in platonic friendship, even if, in some cases she deceives herself. Mrs. Bretton in *Villette*, even though Mrs. Home has but recently died, says sharply "she was as silly and frivolous a little flirt as ever man was weak enough to marry" (chapter 1). Other women of a caustic nature therefore seem to attribute the worst possible motives to any form of charm, but no doubt it served its purpose for calculating flirts and, if the girl in question was a natural charmer, it was perhaps harmless enough.

Another "weapon" could of course be to act exactly like a man and seek to override them in their own field. This, of course, did not go down very well even with the author who usually depicts such women as impossibly arrogant and domineering. Take Rachel Warrington in *The Virginians*. "Little Madam Esmond never came near man or woman but she tried to domineer over them. If people obeyed she was their good friend; if they resisted she fought and fought until she or they gave in. As a mortal, she may have been in the wrong, of course, but she seldom acknowledged the sentiment to herself and to others never" (part 1, chapter 4).

All this sounds like the average strong-willed male—but it evidently wouldn't "do" in one of female sex! Admittedly she had been a spoilt, selfish daughter and an over-strict mother (though if things pleased her, a doting one!). But I am referring to the world of business and estate-management in which she was an expert. Then there is the gentler woman who knows that tears are a way of seeking dependence on the male but through self-discipline refuses to give into them. When Emily's baby dies, she sees that even Arthur weeps (for her as it is her husband, Lopez's child). She cries out: "When one makes up one's mind to that, one does not weep—tears are vain foolish things—when the baby died I cried, but very little (*The Prime Minister,* chapter 59). This may sound hard, but Emily, through suffering brought by the full revelation of her husband's dishonest character, wishes it to be known that she has passed beyond trivial bids for sympathy. On a direct plane, as Sybil has not known the particular grief just described, Egremont admires her because she has "Nothing exaggerated, nothing rhapsodical about her" (chapter 6, book 3). He likewise admires the fact that there is "No affectation of enthusiasm" about her—so many weapons of flattery or winsomeness in general, which Egremont often must meet in Society are wasted on him.

"Weapons," as I've tried to show, are often not more than something used defensively because women had no male prerogatives: viz. Rachel and her "bossiness." But when the weapon is a spontaneous coquettishness, one must remember that firm mothers often fed this attribute as an essential for the marriage stakes. Mind you, a strong personality such as Georgina Longstaffe did not seem to fight for these stakes on the grounds of charm—she felt that rank and striking looks were sufficient. Sadly, that was only in youth. She had "been ten years at the work and was aware she had always flown a little too high for her mark at the time. At nineteen and twenty she had thought all the world was before her. With her commanding figure, regular features and bright complexion she had regarded herself as one of the beauties of the day and had considered herself entitled to demand wealth and a coronet."

Trollope then proceeds satirically through the various stages between nineteen and twenty-nine she has now reached. The satire would perhaps be less ruthless had she not, now, settled for money and a town house although hitherto contemptuous of business Jews. In other words, as male author, he accepts certain methods are employed among ladies seeking a husband, but a loveless marriage chosen deliberately by an intelligent woman and against her father's wishes is another cup of tea altogether (*The Way We Live Now*, chapter 60). At the other end of the social scale but in the same novel, Mrs. Hurtle and Mrs. Pipchin discuss Ruby Ruggles; the former suggests that "in a modern age" girls should be allowed to run after men, as it works the other way on. To which Mrs. Pipchin indignantly retorts: "Anyways, the girls shouldn't be let run after the gentlemen. The gentleman goes here and he goes there and he speaks up free. In my day girls usen't to do that. But then maybe I'm old-fashioned" (chapter 48).

In *The Way We Live Now*, Marie Melmotte develops a "weapon" of her own. She grows businesslike by sheer force of necessity in dealing with her alarming father. Owing to the frightened, much-travelled, shady type of life to which he has exposed her, she allows herself, at first, to be bargained over by two lords whom she dislikes. She then decides to take a hand in her own future (chapter 11) and show her feeling for Felix Carbury. This gives her the courage to speak frankly to her father regarding the money he has put in her name . . . although she knows fully well, of course, this was only for his own dishonest purposes.

When a woman was "herself," it didn't always pay her, as the strong-willed Mrs. Transome was to find out. Thinking over her past, she bitterly comes to the conclusion that "Men like such captives," i.e., those with fire and wit "as they like horses that champ the bit and paw the ground; they feel more triumph in their mastery. What is the use of a woman's will? If she tries, she doesn't get it and she ceases to be loved. God was cruel when he made women" (chapter 39, Felix Holt'). Thus, in her case, her only weapon is useless to her!